RECOVERING *the*
MYSTERY

Recovering *the* MYSTERY

Wittgenstein
Heidegger
Cooper
Dao and Zen

MICHAEL WESTON

à ma petite-fille, Alma.

Contents

Introduction and Overview

'Primitive impressions of existence'

Both Wittgenstein and Heidegger, who will feature largely in
what follows, were readers of Kierkegaard. What I suspect would
have struck them was how he read his *bête-noire* Hegel and the
way this reading was part of a distinctive literary project, that
of the 'pseudonymous authorship'. Kierkegaard didn't engage
Hegel in analysis and criticism of his arguments in order to
replace them with better ones of his own. Rather, he objected
that the very form of Hegel's approach was at odds with what
he claimed to be providing, the 'Truth' which could then inform
the lives of his contemporaries, justified through identifying this
as the self-understanding of Reality itself. (What better source
of justification could there be?, Hegel might ask). Kierkegaard
remarked that a youth who is an 'existing doubter, continually
suspended in doubt... grasps for the truth- so that he can exist
in it.' Here the problem Hegel claims to be addressing is placed
in the *living* context of an individual's life (and who else but an
individual faces this problem, one with their own life?). And
Kierkegaard goes on, ' for an existing person, pure thinking is a
chimera, where the truth is supposed to be the truth in which to
exist' (*Concluding Unscientific Postscript, p. 275*, Oxford, 1992, p. 310).
A philosophy of 'pure thought' presupposes that we stand to the
problem it addresses at a 'theoretical' distance, to be inquired into
and rationally appraised in a disinterested manner to arrive at a
truth binding on all who consider the matter. But, Kierkegaard
pointed out, this is not a relation we can have to our own lives.
We cannot take up a 'disinterested' relation to the meaning of our

lives: rather, the impulse to think one can is itself a manifestation of a particular form of meaningfulness (lived relation to one's existence), *evasiveness*. Any 'theoretical' position is open to further theoretical questioning, so (rationally?) one could postpone indefinitely embarking on any 'answer'. But the individual would still *live*. The idea that such life was 'seeking the Truth' would be merely a superficial gloss on the continuation of their previous existence. Or, half recognizing that one cannot live in hesitation, the individual may think the best they can do is to live in terms of whatever answer presently appears most plausible, but always ready to change. But this is simply a further manifestation of evasiveness, since it fails to reflect the nature of the problem the 'existing doubter' faces, that of their life *as a whole*, which includes any capacity they may have for finding positions plausible or not. The point of the 'pseudonymous authorship', which embodied what Kierkegaard called 'indirect communication', was to provide an opportunity for the reader tempted by this evasiveness to recover a sense of what it is for an existing individual to face this fundamental issue.

Kierkegaard described himself as a 'Christian' writer. His authorship falls into two main categories, the 'direct' and the 'indirect' communications. The direct communications (in his own name), the 'edifying discourses', address fellow Christians, encouraging, strengthening and clarifying their commitment to Christian life. The 'indirect communications' are pseudonymous works which were required because he thought that many 'Christian' lives, those of reflective individuals who were likely to read such works, were lived in illusion as to the nature of Christianity, one which stemmed from a deeper illusion about the nature of their own existence. Such an illusion is not a mistake which can be rectified by giving the one subject to it more knowledge. It is a failure in self-understanding, but not as to some fact relating to their existence (who their biological father is, say). Rather, it is a relation to one's life which exhibits a failure to fully confront the nature of that life, what it is to be a human being. It is an avoidance of one's self, which is, then, *motivated*. As such, the rectification of the illusion must be carried out by the individual themselves, involving a transformation in how they relate to their life. The author of a work of 'indirect communication' is not in the business of providing arguments or persuasions for some position but rather an occasion within which this fundamental recognition by the reader of the nature of their own existence might take place. Kierkegaard says of such an author that he 'stands behind the other man, helping him negatively' so that the 'entire work is repulsion' (*Journals*, 6574). In indirect communication, the communicator disappears, for the recipient must remove her own illusion to be able to be left to herself. 'To stop a man on the street and to stand still in order to speak with him is not as difficult as having to say something to a passerby in passing, without standing still oneself or delaying the other, without wanting to induce him to go the same way, but just urging him to go his own way- and such is the relation between an existing person and an existing person when the communication pertains to the truth as existence-inwardness' (*CUP*, p. 277).

The problem arises out of a person's life as a fundamental, all encompassing, disquiet, one expressed in the first person. It can arise because human life, unlike that of animals, is *accountable* life. Unreflectively we have lived life as 'meaningful': we pursue taken for granted purposes in terms of which we evaluate and judge the situations we find ourselves in or create. This unreflective flow of life is the necessary condition of having a human, accountable life: we must first live unreflectively in order for us to become 'existing doubters', for the question 'what life should I live, and how is this to be determined?' to arise. In this disruptive break the unreflective flow of life appears 'questionable'. This moment of alienation from one's life may be understood by the individual in an illusory way, and this for an evident reason. It may be understood as posing a question which needs to be answered. We may then think we need first to satisfy ourselves as to what the 'Truth' for our life is to be, and only then could we embark on it. As noted above, this understanding is an expression of *evasiveness*, of an unwillingness to face the real nature of the issue. It is this illusion that is embodied in Hegel's approach. The indirect communications are directed towards getting the reader to recognize they are subject to this illusion. *Concluding Unscientific Postscript* and *Philosophical Fragments* not only explicitly (as above) remark on the failure of disinterested inquiry to address the problem faced by the 'existing doubter', but go on to develop an apparently disinterested 'argument' that purports to show that Christian 'truth' is the answer to the 'subjective' problem the doubter faces, as if human life were already constituted as a teleological drive towards Christianity: it's what we always wanted but didn't know it, a 'subjective' repetition of Hegelian dialectic[1]. We readers are entranced by this because, despite apparently taking on board Kierkegaard's stress on the personal, 'subjective' nature of the problem, we now want to interpret this subjective problem as one for disinterested inquiry. We still think we must first satisfy ourselves through such inquiry before we would be willing to embark on living the proposed 'solution'. The *Postscript* therefore ends with a 'Revocation', so that to understand the book is to revoke it, to recognize one's own subjection to the illusion, to attain a self-knowledge. The work does not aim to provide' a little more knowledge a knower can add to his much knowledge but a primitive impression for his existence' (*Concluding Unscientific Postscript*, vol. 2, Oxford, 1992, trans. H. and E. Hong, p. 65).

In revoking the book we may attain a liberation from the alienation from our own lives which the illusion of a 'disinterested' position embodies through recovering a 'primitive impression' of our existence. This 'primitive impression' is a recovery of the situation of the 'existing doubter', an experience of the *lived* nature of the issue. In the 'primitive impression' we recover a sense of the nature of ourselves as existing individuals, and the issue which that existence is for us. We each of us have a relation to our own lives we cannot have to any other. This relation is one of *care*: my life matters to me in a way no other can (my care, or its absence,

---

1. The details of this are not important here. For a detailed treatment, see my paper 'Evading the Issue: the Strategy of Kierkegaard's *Postscript*', *Philosophical Investigations*, vol. 22, no. 1, Jan. 1999, pp. 35-64.

for others is an aspect of my care for my life). Further, *my* life is my *life:* I have a life to live, so that I face, as an 'existing doubter', the issue of relating to my life as a *whole*. I confront my responsibility for taking over my own life. That responsibility cannot be off loaded onto 'the nature of reality' which we must first determine before we can embark on the appropriate life. The illusion of the modern age, Kierkegaard wrote, is to have 'abolished the 'I', the personal 'I'' through making 'everything objective' (*Journals*, 656). I shall look at the possibilities such a responsible individual may face, according to Kierkegaard, in chapter 5.

Kierkegaard was not concerned to develop the possible implications for philosophy more generally of this project of 'indirect communication'. The 'problem of life' manifests itself because human life is *accountable* life. It is a disruption of the meaningful flow of unreflective life within which that life appears as 'questionable'. The problem is, as it were, a moment of alienation, in which we appear to stand over against the flow of our life and ask what its measure may be. It seems to be questionable from an 'external', disinterested position, from which we could ask what could justify it. Within the Western philosophical tradition stemming from Plato, this appears as the question of the 'good life', one which receives a variety of theoretical answers. Characteristically, this takes the form of a reflection on what distinguishes the human from other forms of life and living that distinction in the fullest way will be the most fully human life. And what distinguishes human life is its accountability. The flow of life involves our relating to our environment, to each other, to our pasts and futures, and so forth, a relating which is itself accountable, reflected in the accountability of judgements we may explicitly or implicitly make. Philosophical 'problems' then appear when this taken for granted flow of accountability appears questionable, and we ask whether these taken for granted ways of relating are really justifiable, can issue in true accountability. What we seem to need is a conception of what can provide ultimate justification for human life in all its aspects, a measure for life as a whole. The 'good life' will be life which most fully embodies recognition of this ultimate measure. This 'measure' has appeared variously in Western thought- the Platonic forms, the Ideas in the mind of God, the rational structure of the cosmos, and so forth (Hegel's teleological understanding of Reality as culminating in its own self-understanding in the absolute knowledge embodied in Hegel's thought is only a late development of this). Philosophical 'answers' to the problem of life are thus always an aspect of answering the fundamental question of the measure for life and its experiences as a whole.

But if no such 'disinterested' position is available for an 'existing' individual, the experience of philosophical alienation and what can relieve it must be reconsidered. We need to understand the experience of philosophical alienation in its lived context, not as pointing to the necessity for an external, disinterested position to resolve it, but rather as indicating a failure in self understanding, one which can be remedied by recalling us to ourselves. Philosophical alienation is from unreflective life : we need to see it as requiring a recalling us to the nature of that life, rather than as indicating the necessity for some final viewpoint from which it can be judged. For Wittgenstein and Heidegger, philosophical problems are to be dissolved through recalling us to the nature of unreflective life. Now, in relation to the 'problem of life', as we've seen, Kierkegaard thought it was necessary to recover the 'primitive impression' of existence, that one has to take over one's life for oneself. This 'primitive impression' is then of the 'I', of a self standing over against the world within which life so determined is to be lived. This primitive impression of being a self, however, can arise only out of the flow of unreflective life, in a separation from it, as can the notion of the 'objective'. But then that unreflective flow cannot be characterized in terms of 'self' and a world we stand over against. Wittgenstein and Heidegger recall us rather to a 'primitive impression' of existence prior to the emergence of 'self' and 'other'. As we shall see, this is a recovery of the *mystery* of human life and the world it uncovers. Further, for Heidegger (and I shall suggest arguably for Wittgenstein too) this mystery then appears as the measure for that life, a measure recovered, not in disinterested inquiry, but in a movement of self-understanding. The 'problem of life' disappears in a recovery of how we are anyway in the world. The writings of Wittgenstein's and Heidegger are, then, to be understood as 'indirect communications', directed towards enabling a reader, tempted by the prospect of an illusory disinterested relation to their life, towards that recovery.

Overview

Wittgenstein's *Tractatus* (chapter 1) may appear as a rather forbidding text concerned with addressing 'the nature of logic'. It is certainly that, but Wittgenstein thought that in being such a text it had at the same time an 'ethical', or, indeed, we might say, a 'spiritual', point. The culmination of the text, before its final admonition 'What we cannot speak about we must pass over in silence' (L. Wittgenstein *Tractatus Logico-Philosphicus*, trans. D.F.Pears and B.F.McGuiness, London 1961, proposition 7) which forces us to reflect on the nature of our talk about logic and ethics, lies in the remark 'The solution of the problem of life is seen in the vanishing of the problem' (*Tractatus*, 6.522) and the connection of this to 'things which cannot be put into words. *They make themselves manifest*. They are what is mystical'. The solution of problems with 'the logic of language' is seen in their vanishing, just as the 'problem of life' is resolved in its disappearance. These are, in the *Tractatus*, intimately connected. Philosophical problems have at their root the same 'existential illusion' as underlies the appearance of 'the problem of life', namely thinking that one can occupy an 'external' disinterested position in relation to life in the world from which it can be judged. Then 'logic' appears questionable needing some further 'metaphysical' justification, while life needs to be evaluated in terms of some 'higher' standard. What is needed, rather, is recovery from this illusion. Then we come to 'see the world aright' (*Tractatus*, 6.54), realizing that logic and life stand in no need or possibility of such justification. Then the problems of logic and life disappear. Philosophical self-understanding is one form the removal of existential illusion may take.

Of course, Wittgenstein did not remain content with the *Tractatus*, coming to think that it unwittingly shared in the 'external' theoretical position of traditional philosophy which it thought to have undermined. What was needed was a fuller recognition that the 'urge to understand the foundations' (L. Wittgenstein, *Philosophical Investigations*, trans. G.E.M. Anscombe, P.M.S, Hacker and Joachim Schulte, Oxford 2009,90) is an urge to understand oneself and this required a singular form of communication ('assembling reminders for a particular purpose', 127). It might seem, however, that the Tractarian connection between this form of self understanding and 'the problem of life' is absent in the later writings. I shall, however, propose a way those writings suggest such a connection, even if Wittgenstein himself does not explicitly endorse such a move. The connection lies in recognition of the *mystery* which the dissolution of both philosophical and existential problems requires reference to. The 'urge to understand the foundations' recalls us to ungrounded ways of acting, practices, the viability of which depend on very general conditions both in respect of ourselves and of the world. We realize through this self reflection that our forms of life and the reality they reveal could be otherwise. There is no explanation for why they are as they are, since any explanation could only be in terms of a form of life we find ourselves living. To confront this 'mystery' is 'to be struck by what, once seen, is most striking and most powerful' *(PI 129)*. Wittgenstein does not, I think, follow through, as he had in the *Tractatus*, to draw existential consequences from this, although there is a recorded remark of his that he would prefer 'a change in the way people live' which would make the questions he philosophically addressed 'superfluous' (*Culture and Value*, trans. Peter Winch, Oxford 1980, p. 61e) to a continuation of his work by others. I shall, however, suggest that coming to a self-understanding in terms of 'mystery' leads to an apprehension of how life can appear 'problematic' and how relation to mystery can bring about, as the *Tractatus* proposes, the 'vanishing of the problem' (*T*.6.521). This mystery is not a matter of 'fact', since any 'fact' is the revelation of reality in terms of a form of life. Rather, we may realize, it is for us, living human life, the *source* of the authority which our forms of life have for us, and through that the all encompassing 'authority' in terms of which a meaningful life can be lived. This thought is one we find developed in the work of Martin Heidegger.

Heidegger (chapter 2) sees philosophical questioning as arising out of tendencies fundamental to human existence. I have a life to live, so I have a concern with understanding myself, my capacities and possibilities, and so what kind of being I am. This life is lived in relations to things, both made and unmade by us, and to other people. I must have in this way an understanding of beings in general in terms of which those relations are lived and new situations coped with. I have a concern, then, with 'beings as a whole'. Philosophical questioning is raising this understanding of myself and 'beings as a whole' to explicitness. Such questioning is directed towards self-understanding, towards a self-transformation in which I come to have a transparent understanding of myself and my situation. The concepts developed in this process must recognize this: they are not descriptive concepts of an 'objective reality' (the 'nature of the human being', 'of material being', and so on) but are embedded in a process of self-realization. (Heidegger calls them 'formal indicative' concepts 'which address the challenge of transformation to us but cannot bring it about' (M. Heidegger, *The Fundamental Concepts of Metaphysics*, trans. William McNeill and Nicholas Walker, Bloomington, 1995, p. 296)). The aim of the early writings of Heidegger (up to *Being and Time* and the writings contemporaneous with it) is to provide the occasion for the reader to enter into such a transparent self-understanding and to live accordingly (he calls this 'authentic existence'). In order to fully recognize that the reflection is by an individual about their own lives, we need to find the impetus to develop philosophical questioning *within* individual life itself. Heidegger does this by reference to *breaks* in the flow of unreflective life which open up the vista, as it were, within which the nature of our environing world and of our lives as a whole are available for reflective appropriation. In this, we realize that the *primordial* way in which beings are revealed is in unreflective life, in the flow of purposive concerned life living within an environing world. They are not primordially revealed as 'objects' for a 'representing subject' but as the familiar furniture of our concernful living. Through this reflective appropriation of ourselves and our world opened up by breaks in the flow of this life, we confront our 'finitude': that we are 'thrown' into our finite lives, with their particular capacities and abilities, within a given historical situation. In everyday life we inhabit this finitude without taking an explicit stand in relation to it. Our reflection enables us to do just this. We are able to take over our finitude by 'resolute choice' and so live life as 'my own': I take over affirmatively my mortality, my given nature and my historical situation by choosing my 'hero', a model life suggested by or developed from tradition.

The later writings see this notion of finitude as too restrictive and so what it is to live one's finitude changes accordingly. We need to be drawn back to recognize the 'givenness' of our nature as revealing beings and so to the 'givenness' of what is manifest in the flow of life. Beings are indeed familiar, revealed in our life and the concepts derived from our concerns, and yet in their authority for us (they are *beings*, a standard for our thoughts and actions), in their givenness, they embody concealment, a mystery. They are familiar and *other*. This derives from the mystery of the givenness of our nature as revealing what is (there need have been no such human revelation, and that there is gives us a way *to be*, it is a life which can be lived more or less well). It is this mystery, of the giving of human life and the world that life reveals, which is itself concealed increasingly in the ways in which the nature of human life and the world have been thought in the history of Western culture, which Heidegger calls 'the History of Being'. This history unfolds as a progressive attempt to repress mystery, to make human life and the world 'present' to our representation. Its hold on us is broken when this repression takes a turn against presence as representation and releases a vision of life and the world as 'resources' for endless remaking. The history is revealed as history, and so opening us to an experience of the mystery of the givenness of human life as revealing what is, even as 'resource'. Now to take over our finitude is not to live the authentic life of resolute choice, but 'releasement' to the mystery, a life which puts mystery as its centre. The mystery is, and I shall note later Heidegger's emphasis on this, transhistorical and transcultural, opening up the possibility of his engagement with East Asian thought.

Heidegger diagnoses the fundamental philosophical 'attunement' as 'homesickness', the need to be 'at home everywhere' (*FCM*p. 5). For us, life is an issue, so the kind of life we lead is potentially a question, and one which therefore requires us to be *accountable*. The life we take on cannot be justified by appeal to our desires and inclinations as they are part of what is to be accounted for. We need a *measure* beyond ourselves. Further, that life is life in the world, and our general beliefs and understandings of that world must themselves be warranted if our lives are to have the significance we claim for them. There is, then, an impetus within human life towards some measure of accountability in terms of which the human and the world can be unified, some way in which we can be 'at home' in the world so that it is the sort of world within which a worthwhile life may be lived. David Cooper (chapter 3), whose writings provide, as we shall see, a wide-ranging defence of according to mystery the central role in this, calls such understandings 'visions'. Visions are not themselves accountable, seen from within, from the perspective of someone who lives them, since they provide the forms which accountability can take. The various 'epochs' of Heidegger's History of Being can be seen as such 'visions': they provide the available conceptual understanding of accountability at various times in terms of an overall vision of the unity of human life with the world. (Heidegger's notion of 'epochs' does not refer to temporal periods but to the way the sequence of 'epochs' are responses to the 'withdrawal', the concealing, of mystery). Cooper himself provides a sketch of a sequence of such visions from the Medieval Augustinian to the 'existential humanism' of the early Heidegger. The central issue here for Cooper is the nature of the measure in terms of which the human can be united with their world. In the European tradition, this has taken two broad forms. One is to see the measure lying in 'reality as it any way is', independent of any reference to human life. The Platonic Forms, the *logos* of the *kosmos* in Aristotle, the Augustinian understanding of the world and the human as creations according to the Ideas in the mind of God, are examples of this, as too is the later conception of our living in a 'rational world', one whose intelligible structure is (whether through Divine gift or simply as the most general 'fact') comprehensible by us. The difficulties in holding to such conceptions, which are ever likely to give rise to skeptical doubts (how can we know we have access to the way things really are, given this is understood as independent conceptually of human life?), gives rise to attempts to form such a 'vision' in terms of human life itself, abandoning the notion of 'reality as it any way is'. The world we inhabit is understandable solely in terms of concepts embedded in human practices which are expressions of our purposes and interests. But put bluntly like that, we seem to have the familiar problem: how can human life and its understanding of the world justify itself? 'Uncompensated humanism' Cooper says is unlivable: in order to find our lives significant and our understandings of the world firmly grounded we need to refer to beyond human life itself: but not to 'reality as it any way is', which has been shown to fail to accomplish this mission. Any world we can describe is indeed one formed in terms of human purposes and interests, but, Cooper suggests, we must refer this to a 'beyond' which is not discursable, to 'mystery'. We must then regard ourselves and the world as 'given'.

But this is not a once and for all 'creation'. It is a mysterious *giving* which constitutes the primordial way beings are revealed in our unreflective purposive lives. We need to recover the nature of the unreflective flow of life because it is there we find the fundamental way in which we and the reality we uncover are bound together and experienced as *given*. (It is to the flow of life that Wittgenstein recalls us in order to dissolve philosophical problems: 'Only in the stream of life and thought do words have meaning' (L. Wittgenstein *Zettel*, trans. G.E.M. Anscombe and G.H. von Wright, Oxford, 1967, 173)). The nature of this primordial way lights up for us in 'epiphanies', experiences which show the nature of experience itself. Reflections on water are an example (Cooper has written a brief and fascinating book on the significance of such reflections, *Sunlight on the Sea*, (no place of publication given), 2013). What we see is not independent of our conceptual and physical capacities, yet we are 'inscribed' by the reflection, we are receptive, it 'presences'. To recognize this 'giving' of ourselves as receptive and the reality inscribed in us is to recognize our 'convergence with the world'. In primordial experience, there is no separation of 'self' and 'object': there is only the seamless arising of reality. Such separation arises in breaks in the flow of life, where we need to take stock, make decisions, and so forth. 'Homelessness', however, results from taking the separation of 'self' and 'object' as primary, forgetting its dependence on convergence, and then attempting to recover a sense of unity through domestication, control of the field of alien 'objects', an attempt which must fail.

What then is life like when we recognize primordial convergence, the mystery of the arising of human life in its uncovering of reality, and take this mystery as the measure? Cooper finds a resource here in East Asian thought (he has written a book (*Convergence with Nature*, Totnes, 2012) suggesting a Daoist perspective on the natural world). I turn then in Chapter 4 to a discussion of some central Daoist and Zen texts.

Life for the human being is an issue as they have a life to live, rather than just living as (one may suppose) animals do. But what is the nature of this 'issue'? One way it may appear is as a question to be answered by the formation of a pattern of the 'good life' to aim for, so that the living 'I', for whom the issue arises, projects forward a future 'self'. (As noted above, Western philosophy characteristically asks after the good life for the human being, and determines it in terms of humanity's 'essential' difference from other beings. The life most fully expressing this difference will be the most human life and the one to aim for.) For Daoism and Zen this response is itself a manifestation of what has gone wrong with life to produce the 'issue'. The 'problem' of life is not to be solved but to disappear. The *Dao De Jing* remarks that whereas the pursuit of learning (as for example in the philosophical response above) 'is to increase day after day', the pursuit of Dao 'is to decrease day after day' (chapter 48, translated Keping Wang, *Reading the Dao*, London, 2011, p. 160). And the Zen master Dogen writes 'To study the way of enlightenment is to study the self. To study the self is to forget the self' (*The Essential Dogen*, ed. Kazuaki Tanahashi and Peter Levitt, Boston, 2013, p. 53). The 'problem' of life arises with the arising of the 'self', distinguished from the 'other' of the world, which the living 'I' then sees as its goal. But this involves not merely a separation of 'self' from 'world', but a self-alienation, an internal division within the 'I' for whom the issue arises. The living 'I' sees its 'real self' as lying in a projected future, and it is this self-alienation which is the nature of the 'issue', of the problem with life. The problem disappears when the separation of the 'I' from itself and from the world disappears in a recognition of the primordial unity of living life and world which constitutes how we are unreflectively. Of course, reflection is perfectly legitimate, and with it an arising of 'self' and 'object', in breaks in the flow of life, in moments of taking stock and decision, provided it is recognized that these are exceptional moments dependent for their intelligibility on the flow of life rather than indicating the nature of reality itself. It is the taken for granted understanding of the world in terms of 'self' and 'other', of a subject confronting a world of 'objects' in pursuit of a future 'self', that produces a problem of life to be solved. What is needed rather is to recover, reflectively, the primacy of the unity of living life and the world. The pursuit of Dao is to decrease every day the hold of the alienating self-understanding on the living 'I', just as the 'study of enlightenment' is to 'forget the self'.

In forgetting the self, we forget the 'other' which conceptually depends on it. As Dogen goes on to say, 'To forget the self is to be actualized by myriad beings' (ibid.) and the Daoist sage Chuang-tzu quotes 'heaven and earth were born together with me, the myriad things and I are one' (A.C.Graham, *Chuang-tzu: The Inner Chapters*, Indianapolis, 2001, p. 56). In the primordial flow of life, which is always in the first person, there is no separation of 'self' and 'other', only the constant arising of 'myriad things'. It is the *giving* of this which we reflectively realize when we 'pursue Dao' or 'study the way of enlightenment'. The 'issue' of life disappears when we (the living 'I') explicitly embrace the giving of the flow of life. Hence the life of one who pursues Dao or 'studies' enlightenment is one of profound receptivity, openness to what is given, and of action as a giving without a goal, 'roaming without destination' as the Daoist maxim has it.

Recognition of the giving of the 'I' and the world determines the 'temporality' of the sage's or Zen master's life. The life of the dualistic self, of the 'I' which has objectified itself as a 'self' to be achieved, is oriented towards what happens in the future. The past is done with, as what has happened, while the present presents objects to be utilized in the pursuit of the 'self'. Past, present and future are here relative terms, having sense in relation to each other. But the sage or Zen master lives explicitly in the 'timeless present' of the giving of the flow of life itself. The sage lives in the 'undying' (Graham,p. 87), while the Zen master lives in the 'absolute now', *nikon*. As Dogen says, 'when timelessness is realized, you are alive' (*ED*, p. 94), for that is the very nature of the living 'I' which is repressed in the search for a self: 'the time right now is all there ever is' (ibid.). The issue of life disappears when we come back to who we always already are, the living 'I' which is the arising of 'myriad things'.

The sayings of these texts are not 'statements of doctrine' but rather 'reminders' to prompt us to an undistorted recollection of the primordial way we are in the world and with others. Their vocabulary is essentially negative: in Zen, 'emptiness' (of the projections of 'self' and 'other'), not-self (*anatman*), Buddha-nature (not the nature projected by 'self', by 'discriminating mind'), and in Daoism the *wu*-forms such as *wu-wei* (non-action, action which arises spontaneously in life lived for itself without a goal), *wu-yu* (non-desire, the desire which characterizes such life), and so on. I will discuss these forms in chapter 4.

The progress of this discussion has taken us very far from its beginnings in Kierkegaard, and so the first task in Chapter 5 will be to address the differences between his understanding of the 'issue' of life faced by the individual with that we find in Daoism and Dogen's Zen. I shall suggest that Kierkegaard's Christianity is an 'infinitizing' of the 'self', in which the individual aims at the absolute division between herself and the world which is conformity with the 'will' of God, the divine creator. Kierkegaard's separate 'I' is always to be achieved by 'dropping away' the world, holding before herself transformation into 'eternal life', whereas for Daoism and Zen it is just this sense of 'self' which is to be 'dropped away'. If the latter, in pursuing Dao or in 'forgetting the self', embody, as I will suggest, a 'vision of mystery', while Kierkegaard's Christianity does not, the question arises of the relation between such a 'vision' and religion more generally (chapter 5).

David Cooper has suggested that mystery is 'the *default* ' mode of experiencing the world and life (*The Measure of Things* Oxford, 2007, p. 346), and that in 'the absence of theoretical conceptions, whether of a primitive or sophisticated type, the world would be experienced as a grace-given epiphany' (ibid. p. 347). Since non-revealed religions appear to be replete with gods, spirits and other 'supernatural' beings, it might seem that they occlude such an epiphany. How are we to understand the nature of such 'beings' if not as 'theoretical' conceptions introduced in order to explain life and the world?

I take up here Wittgenstein's discussion of Frazer's *The Golden Bough* ('Remarks on Frazer's *Golden Bough*' in Ludwig Wittgenstein *Philosophical Occasions 1912-1951*, ed. James Klagge and Alfred Nordmann, Indianapolis 1993) which articulates such an understanding of 'divine' beings. Frazer's account presupposes that religion is engaged in an 'explanatory' project which we realize is rightfully superseded by science. Wittgenstein objects that the ritual practices and associated beliefs Frazer discusses are not to be seen as an extension of the already extensive technological knowledge and expertise of the peoples concerned. I take up the trajectory of Wittgenstein's discussion by raising the question how we identify practices and beliefs as 'religious'. We learn the term, of course, in relation to specific practices and beliefs, but we can and do naturally extend the understanding to new and unfamiliar cases. I look here at a specific example, of specialists in Andean cultures identifying practices and material remains of the Moche culture as 'religious'. The Moche, a culture extant on the northern coast of Peru between the first and the eighth centuries of the Common Era, were not literate and there is no continuity of culture into the time of the entry of literate people into the area, so we have no access to what the Moche said about their practices and the beliefs associated with them. What, then, informs the interpretations of modern specialists in their identifying practices, sites and material remains as 'religious'? I examine interpretations of ritual human sacrifice and sexual activity to uncover the dimension of human life these interpreters naturally appeal to in order to make sense of the available data. I suggest this bears out Wittgenstein's remark that 'The form of the awakening spirit is veneration' (ibid.p.139), and that we are to understand this veneration as directed towards the mysterious giving of life and the world. It is in this connection that we are to understand the notions of 'supernatural beings' and the 'mythological' discourses in which they figure (although, of course, we do not have these for the Moche).

I then take up the nature of such discourses, the question of the temporality involved in so-called 'Creation' 'myths', and the nature of the 'beings' involved in them, in relation to indigenous Australian conceptions of 'The Dreaming' and 'Ancestral Spirits', and in relation to Egyptian myth and its apparent bewildering proliferation of 'divine beings'. I suggest, in their respective understandings of the 'arising' of 'ancestral spirits' and of the gods, and the nature of the temporality involved in this, these religions do indeed participate in the 'vision of mystery'. I suggest that 'gods' and 'spirits' are the way the authority of forms of life and the reality they reveal is articulated from *within* living those forms of life. The focus is not on their 'arising' as what gives them their divinity, not on 'mystery' as the ultimate source of authority for human life and the reality it reveals, although this is implicit in their conceptions of 'gods' or 'ancestral spirits'.

The Daoist, Zen and Western philosophical texts I have considered, however, are concerned with a *recovery* of something which has been lost. The Daoist texts address those who have 'lost the Way' and Dogen's those who are mired in the illusions of 'discriminating mind', while Heidegger traces the long history of the West in losing touch with the source of all authority in mystery, culminating in the illusion of the human as its own source. Their writings are directed towards getting the reader to identify their own illusions or those of their culture and start on the way to a recovery, towards a self-understanding which is an understanding of who they always already were, as mysteriously *given*. The language of these authors is informed by this, to recall us to an undistorted apprehension of the primordial way we are in the world and with others. They do not therefore develop 'doctrines', but rather give us 'reminders for a particular purpose' (Wittgenstein), try to open us to an 'experience' of 'Appropriation' (Heidegger), or try to liberate us from the language of 'self' and 'other' through the negative vocabulary of Zen and Daoism. As Wittgenstein remarked in the *Tractatus*, the 'solution of the problem of life is seen in the vanishing of the problem' (6.521), and it vanishes in the recovery of our primordial way of being, in our reconnection with mystery.

Chapter 1

Wittgenstein: from 'the mystical'
to the mystery of the everyday.

Both the early (*Tractatus*) and the later (*Philosophical Investigations*)
Wittgenstein see philosophical problems, and so their purported
resolutions, as the result of a 'misunderstanding' of the 'logic of
our language' (*T* Preface), a 'misunderstanding of the logic of
language' (*PI* 93). This 'misunderstanding' is of how that logic
may be articulated, how it may reflectively appear. 'Logical
investigation explores the essence of all things. It seeks to see to
the foundation of things' (*PI* 89)...our investigation is directed
not towards *phenomena*, but rather, as one might say, towards the
'possibilities' of phenomena' (*PI* 90). This 'urge to understand the
foundations' (*PI* 89) involves a break with the flow of everyday
life, reflectively turning on it to ask after its 'possibility'. Within
everyday life, we relate to others, to our environments, engage
in discussions with others and with ourselves about what has
occurred or may happen, and so forth, in a way which is
untroubled, matter of course: we raise issues and resolve them in
a taken for granted, shared manner. In a fundamental reflective
mode, we may ask how it is possible for us to know people, our
familiar environments and the wider world, to have access to what
is not present, the past, or project into the future on the basis of
what has occurred in that past. And, at the most fundamental
level, we may wonder how we can have any relation to reality at
all. What makes possible our statements about the world which
can be true or false, or wishes or orders that wish and order that
things be thus and so? Wittgenstein neither early or late wished

to denigrate this 'urge to understand the foundations', but rather to show that philosophy misunderstands how that urge is to be satisfied, what sort of articulation is appropriate to revealing the 'foundations' of our everyday lives to us. It fails to reflect on *how* its problems arise, and so what is appropriate to remove them. Philosophy sees its 'problems ' as revealing problems *with* our everyday life, something amiss with our unreflective life with each other and with the world which requires philosophical resolution in the light of which our everyday lives must undergo change. The problems are in this way an expression of an *alienation* from the certainty with which we live our everyday life. This perception of philosophical 'problems' as ones *with* life requires the philosopher to attain, as it were, a position from which everyday life can be held to account, an 'external' viewpoint on life and the reality with which it engages. Wittgenstein both early and late sees this position as an illusion, as, therefore, are the problems that it claims to see and the theories proposed to resolve them. But this is not to say that the 'urge to understand the foundations' is equally invalid. This reflective move for Wittgenstein is not an alienation from life but rather one towards self-understanding, requiring, not a fantastical external position on life and reality, but one which recognizes that the philosopher is inextricably within that life which she tries to reflectively appropriate. As Wittgenstein put it in *PI*: 'the real foundations of their inquiry do not strike people at all. Unless *that* fact has at some time struck them.-And this means: we fail to be struck by what, once seen, is most striking and most powerful" (129). How to bring about that reflective awareness is what is at issue throughout Wittgenstein's work. But, as we shall see, the later Wittgenstein came to think his earlier self in the *T* had been complicit with the fantasy of an 'external position' on life and thought even while believing himself to be revealing its illusory nature. What is of central concern in the present context, however, is that the *T*, although affirming that 'all the propositions of our everyday language, just as they stand, are in perfect logical order' (*T* 5563), nevertheless sees the move in which the illusory nature of traditional philosophical problems appears, as revealing at the same time 'the solution of the problem of life' in its vanishing. The internal reflective move of the *T* has an *ethical or existential point*. The internal self-understanding of the *T* is at the same time a self-revelation, one which shows certain dominant existential positions implicitly lived in everyday life to be themselves illusions if they are understood as giving meaning to life as a whole. In this way, the illusory position from which philosophical problems are seen appears as an intellectual manifestation of an existential illusion. After outlining the way the *T* tries to get us to this realization, I want to ask: can the same be said for the reflective understanding which appears in the later work, or does its critical relation to the *T* extend to the latter's existential implications?

1) The Tractatus.

In a letter to Russell (19 August, 1919, quoted in W. Child, *Wittgenstein*, London, 2011,p. 61), Wittgenstein explained that 'the main point' of the *Tractatus* 'is the theory of what can be expressed (*gesagt*) by propositions-i.e. by language- (and, which comes to the same thing, what can be *thought*) and what cannot be expressed by propositions, but only shown (*gezeigt*); which, I believe, is the cardinal problem of philosophy'. In the preface to the *Tractatus*, Wittgenstein tells us that the 'problems of philosophy', with which the book deals, are 'posed...(because) the logic of our language is misunderstood. The whole sense of the book might be summed up in the following words: what can be said at all can be said clearly, and what we cannot talk about we must pass over in silence' (p. 3). The 'misunderstanding' of logic which provokes the posing of traditional problems of philosophy is that logic can be formulated in propositions. Rather, logic *shows* itself in the formulation and application of propositions. The aim of the *Tractatus* (hereafter *T*) the Preface continues, is 'to set a limit to thought, or rather-not to thought, but to the expression of thoughts: for in order to be able to set a limit to thought, we should have to find both sides of the limit thinkable (that is, we should have to be able to think what cannot be thought).

It will therefore only be in language that the limit can be set, and what lies on the other side of the limit will simply be nonsense' (p.3). To 'set a limit to thought', to demarcate what is intelligible from what is not, cannot be carried out as if we occupied an *external* position to thought. It is precisely this which prompts traditional philosophical problems: the idea that we can stand in a representational relation to thought and so formulate logic in propositions. This provokes the attempt to *ground*, to find a justification for, the logic which manifests itself in our ordinary propositional behaviour, since the external position of representing seems to suggest that the logic we are observing could have been otherwise, as a proposition can be either true or false. We need, therefore, a justification for why it is the way it is (say, by appeal to Platonic Ideas or Ideas in the mind of God). To say with Wittgenstein that 'logic must look after itself' (*T* 5.473) is to say that it can have no justification and so the raising of such a question and any formulation of 'answers' must only produce nonsense. Revealing the logic of our language can only be done internally to language in such a way that it is shown rather than expressed in propositions. Philosophy in the Tractarian sense is 'not a body of doctrine but an activity.

A philosophical work consists essentially of elucidations (*Erlauterungen*)" (*T*.4.112). The activity of philosophy lies neither in producing propositions peculiar to itself nor in producing non-philosophical propositions as is proper to ordinary life. Rather, it lies in addressing the latter, not in use, but in allowing their logic to display itself. 'Without philosophy thoughts are, as it were, cloudy and indistinct: its task is to make them clear and to give them sharp boundaries' (*T* 4.112). It does this first through formulating propositions in a perspicuous symbolism which makes clear the logical role of the elements of the proposition, so that 'Now, too, we understand our feeling that once we have a sign language in which everything is all right, we already have a correct logical point of view' (*T* 4.1213), and then by setting out the truth conditions of the complex propositions of everyday and scientific life. This analysis must terminate if sense is to be determinate, and the propositions which bring it to an end, elementary propositions, must be unanalysable in this way and so be logically independent of each other. In setting out propositions in an adequate symbolism and in giving their truth functional analysis, we display the logic of our language, of our thought. 'Thus one proposition '*fa*' shows that the object *a* occurs in its sense, two propositions '*fa*' and '*ga*' show that the same object is mentioned in both of them. If two propositions contradict one another, then their structure shows it; the same is true if one of them follows from the other. And so on'. (*T* 4.1211). And 'What *can* be shown, *cannot* be said' (*T* 4.1212). What is shown in formulating propositions in an adequate symbolism and in their truth functional analysis cannot itself be formulated in propositions, cannot be 'said', since what is shown is what makes a proposition, as a representation of what it is about, possible. A proposition, as such a saying, is either true or false, whereas putative formulations of the logic of language would not have true-false polarity. They would not 'say' (represent) anything.

'Elucidation' is showing. Elementary propositions cannot be analysed truth functionally; they are 'truth functions of themselves'. Their signs are, therefore, primitive and cannot be defined. The meaning of such primitive signs must be shown and cannot be verbally explained. 'The meanings of primitive signs can be explained by means of elucidation. Elucidations are propositions that contain the primitive signs. So they can only be understood if the meanings of those signs are already known' (*T* 3.263). This is something shown in the ordinary use of propositions, since any such complex propositions presuppose the meaningfulness of the primitive signs of the elementary propositions which would terminate their truth functional analysis. Elucidation here is simply showing elementary propositions as elementary, and primitive signs as primitive, in terminating the logical analysis of a complex proposition and its complex signs, and so as meaning in a way that precludes definition. The meaning of the primitive signs must, in formulating ordinary propositions, have been simply grasped, just as we must see, in an unmediated form, what a painted picture is a picture of.

Of course, the *Tractatus* itself appears to 'say' what it claims can only be shown, and indeed this claim itself appears unsayable. Its 'propositions' do not have true-false polarity. 'My propositions serve as elucidations in the following way: anyone who understands me eventually recognizes them as nonsensical, when he has used them-as steps- to climb beyond them. (He must, so to speak, throw away the ladder after he has climbed up it). He must transcend these propositions, and then he will see the world aright' (*T* 6.54). Elucidations are uses of propositions, not to state something, but to allow something about those propositions to show itself. The 'propositions' of the *Tractatus* lack true-false polarity and so are 'nonsense'. But they are a use of such apparent propositions precisely to direct us to the distinction between propositions and what they state, on the one hand, and what is shown in their use, on the other, the distinction between what can be said and what can only be shown. In that sense, the *'propositions'* of the *Tractatus* are elucidations: they show showing, as it were. Since we cannot understand these 'propositions' as propositions, we have to understand the authorial intention of producing them ('understand me') in order to see their elucidatory function. They elucidate, show, the showing in the said, by a sort of parody of traditional philosophical propositions. Such a use of 'propositions' is directed towards undermining the apparent external position from which they would seem to issue, revealing the illusory nature of such a position and gaining us the realization that the clarification of 'logic' is a form of self-understanding on the part of the inquirer.

In a letter to Ludwig Fricker, a potential publisher of the *Tractatus*, Wittgenstein wrote that 'The book's point is an ethical one'. It has two parts, the written and the unwritten, and it is the latter which is important. It is this part which 'draws limits to the sphere of the ethical from the inside as it were, and, I am convinced that this is the *only* rigorous way of drawing these limits'. And he then draws Fricker's attention to the Preface and the conclusion of the work 'because they contain the most direct expression of the point of the book" (P.Engelman, *Letters from Ludwig Wittgenstein*, Oxford, 1967, pp143-4, quoted Child p. 61). As we have seen, the Preface states the book's aim as 'drawing a limit to thought' which can only be done from within language, but the implication of the remark in the letter to Fricker is that this is at the same time drawing 'limits to the sphere of the ethical'. How is this?

A proposition in the T is a set of physical marks or sounds arranged according to rules in terms of which it is a 'picture' of a possible state of affairs. We read the sense immediately off the propositional sign just as we see what is represented in a picture. The world as the world of facts is a world which essentially can be stated in propositions. The logic of language is at the same time the logic of the world. Propositions are sign pictures in use to represent the world, and so presuppose the 'I' who pictures, represents. This 'I' is not part of the world of facts but a presupposition of there being a world which is essentially statable. 'The world is *my* world, this is manifest in the fact that the limits of language mean the limits of my world' (T 5.62). There is no conception of the world other than that given in language: I have world in being the 'I' that speaks language and so relates to the world. (All languages are in this sense one, their differences purely conventional. They all give 'world', and this, like 'language', does not have a plural). The 'I' presupposed by the world, the 'I' which thinks and so relates to the world is not part of the world. 'There is no such thing as the subject that thinks or entertains ideas' (T 5.631). 'The subject does not belong to the world: rather, it is a limit of the world' (T 5.632). 'The philosophical self is not the human being, not the human body, or the human soul, with which psychology deals, but rather the metaphysical subject, the limit of the world-not part of it' (*T* 5.641). The phenomenal self, the dispositions, capacities bodily and mental, emotions, desires, and so forth which distinguish human beings, one from another, is part of the world. The 'I' which is a condition of the world rather than a part of it is the 'I' presupposed by a world which essentially can be stated, a world of facts. This 'I' is we might say *living* life, which is a relating to the world of facts (to other facts through relating to the facts of the phenomenal self). This life can be 'happy' or 'unhappy' (*T* 6.43). The 'unhappy life' is one for which 'the problem of the meaning of life' exists and is to be *answered* (as the 'unhappy logician' is one for whom logical problems exist and are to be answered rather than dissolved). The 'problem of life' is the problem of the *measure* for life, what is it that gives meaning to life. The unhappy life seeks to answer this by finding some measure to which the world is answerable: in terms of this measure, 'facts' become discriminated as 'good', 'bad', 'indifferent', and so forth. Such discrimination then leads to the 'unhappy life' being frustrated, disappointed, or of course pleased, by the world. The idea of such an 'external measure' is, however, an illusion. There is no external position from which the world can be subject to judgement. Rather, the measure for the world, the 'totality of facts' (*T*, 1.1), shows itself in the showing of its possibility. The world is the world of facts, facts are what can be thought or stated, and so presuppose the 'I' which thinks. This 'I' is not part of the world of facts but its presupposition, and so the 'happy' life fully recognizes and accepts that 'in the world everything is as it is, and everything happens as it does happen: in it no value exists' (*T* 6.41), and so that the 'world is independent of my will' (*T* 6.373). 'All propositions are of equal value' (*T.* 6.4). Such a life relates to the world as a whole (facts as such) and so to life as a whole in the world by fully accepting the independence of the world (of facts as facts). This is to live in such a way that nothing that occurs can frustrate or indeed satisfy the 'I'. Whatever occurs is willed by the 'I' which wills the independence of the world and so fully accepts the world as the world of facts. What is willed by the happy I is so independently of what may occur: it is willed 'for its own sake'. This is living in the 'present' since the willing of an action or project is not dependent on expected or hoped for consequences in the world. To live in the present is to live in terms of the timeless or the 'eternal': 'eternal life belongs to those who live in the present' (*T* 6.4311). The life of the 'I' which is a condition of the world and not part of it lives in the present, and so always in relation to the timeless which is *sense*. Propositional signs have sense in picturing possible situations. Logical form in terms of the possible logical relations of complex propositions and the situations they picture, and of the possible elementary propositions and the states of affairs they picture, is timeless, the condition for there being facts in time, the world of the temporal. In living in terms of the timeless, the eternal, the 'I' lives in terms of sense: its actions and projects are willed in terms of their sense, their description alone, and it formulates propositions whose possibility is independent of what is the case. The unhappy self is, then, one which does not live in terms of self-knowledge and so of its independence of the world and the world's independence of it. The will of the unhappy self is conditional upon projected happenings in the world; what it wills has conditional rather than the absolute value of the happy self. The unhappy self lives in terms of the illusion of a position from which the world could be judged.

Philosophical illusion arises from imagining an external position to reality (and so to life) in which the normative dimension of our ordinary life with propositions (that propositions have sense and stand in inferential relations with other propositions) appears as a 'fact' and so requires justification as to its normativity. The strategy of the *Tractatus* ('understand me') is to dispel this illusion: to get us to see that the logic of language is displayed, shown, in the formation and application of propositions. This 'showing' can be made perspicuous through formulating propositions in an adequate symbolism and by setting out their truth-functional analysis, through an activity rather than a doctrine. But there is nothing inadequate in our everyday use of propositions. 'In fact, all the propositions of our everyday language, just as they stand, are in perfect logical order' (*T* 5563). The point of philosophy is to allow this logical order to show itself in a perspicuous way. The order, however, is always present as hidden in our everyday understanding: 'If we know on purely logical grounds that there must be elementary propositions, then everyone who understands propositions propositions in their unanalyzed form must know it' (*T* 5562).

The 'ladder' of the *Tractatus* 'ascends' to the final entries on the ethical and the meaning of life. *Philosophical illusion is to be shown as a particular (intellectual) form of existential illusion.* Philosophical illusion is the result of a failure to recognize that the philosopher cannot presume to ascend to a position from which the world and life can be judged, submitted to an external standard of intelligibility. The (supposed) formulation of such a position and its standards results only in nonsense. Rather, to see the world and life *sub specie aeternitatis* is to see them, not externally but, from within life itself, in terms of the present.

The intelligibility of the world of facts appears as the presence of the timeless *sense* of propositions we formulate in our everyday lives independent of their truth or falsity. The relation to the world of the 'I' which formulates propositions appears as full recognition of the independence of the world of facts (and so of propositions as about 'reality', as having truth-falsity polarity). The I therefore wills actions and projects independently of their consequences in the world, living in terms of 'absolute' rather than 'conditional' value. (Of course, it remains a problem to understand how these actions and projects are to be carried out in the world, as this will is not the phenomenal will in the world but that of the 'I' which is a condition of there being a world at all). The unhappy individual assumes an 'external' position to the world in projecting value on it, so that the value of life lies in 'valuable' consequences in the world. Indeed, the philosophical projection of value on the world characteristic of traditional philosophical resolutions to the 'problem' of the significance of life (in terms, for example, of teleology), is just an intellectual form of this. 'The solution of the problem of life is seen in the vanishing of the problem' (*T* 6.521). The only intelligible questions are ones with answers and these concern the truth and falsity of propositions about the world (*T* 6.52). To experience the 'problem' of life is to fail to recognize the independence of the world and so the independence of the 'I' which is a condition of the world. When the independence of the 'I' is recognized the relation to the world in terms of 'absolute' value is itself given. Then, having ascended the ladder of the 'propositions' of the *Tractatus*, recognizing what is shown by our life in the world, we 'will see the world aright', we will see the world and our lives from within, in terms of the present. Philosophical illusion and the 'problem' of life will be dispelled.

It is this which underlies the notion of the 'mystical' in the *T*:

6.44 It is not *how* things are in the world that is mystical, but that it exists.

6.45 To view the world *sub specie aeterni* is to view it as a whole- a limited whole.

Feeling the world as a limited whole- it is this which is mystical. The world is the world of facts, the totality of what is pictured by true propositions, and this depends on the totality of possible propositions, the totality of sense. The world is viewed as a 'whole-a limited whole' when viewed from the 'eternal', which is the *timeless present*. The view of the eternal is not an external perspective on the temporal world of facts, but the position of the 'I' which wills and formulates propositions in terms of sense alone: 'eternal life belongs to those who live in the present' (6.4311). When we are divested of the illusion of the external position which produces 'problems of logic' and the 'problem of life', this is how the world and the self appear, in the light of the 'eternal', the timeless present. One understands oneself as the 'I' of the timeless present relating to the totality of the world of facts (including those of the 'psychological self') through the totality of sense. The 'mystical' is the appearance of the self and world in terms of the eternal present. It is to this vision that the structure of the *T* is directed. We come to see the 'propositions' produced by the illusion of an external position as lacking sense, while still engaged on the project that this illusion was meant to address, understanding the justifiability of propositions and of life. This culminates in the vision of the mystical, in how the self and world appear in the timeless present. Divested of illusion, we can *live* in the present, live 'eternal life'. The world of the 'happy' I is, one might say, a 'mystical world'. The final proposition of the *T*, 'What we cannot speak about we must pass over in silence' (proposition 7) points to the release from the illusion of the external position from which life and the world may be judged. We cannot speak *about* 'life' and the 'world'. Rather, we can speak about 'states of affairs' in the world (which, if they exist, are 'facts'), and can formulate expressions of will within life. But the nature of life and the world *shows itself* in life lived without illusion, eternal life, life beyond justification, life lived for itself.

2) *The Philosophical Investigations.*

For the *Tractatus*, the logic of our language cannot be stated, represented, as if from an external position, but shows itself perspicuously in the truth functional analysis of our everyday propositions which terminates in elementary propositions which are logically independent and must therefore be grasped independently of explanation (understood as analysis). This 'immediate grasp' is analogous to the way we see immediately what a picture represents, and indeed both the picture and the propositional sign can be grasped in this way because they share logical form. All pictures, propositional or otherwise, are logical pictures. All explanation, all interpretation, must come to an end in what cannot be explained or interpreted, and there we must simply grasp what is pictured, what is meant. As *PI* 95 expresses this inclination: 'when we say, mean, that such-and-such is the case, then, with what we mean, we do not stop anywhere short of the fact, but mean *such-and-such-*

is-so-and-so'. The logical picture shows us the situation whose existence would make it true. The proposition as logical picture therefore has the form ' This is how things stand': it is a picture which claims to show the way things are (unlike pictures, say, illustrating a work of fiction, or genre paintings). We understand the proposition as a picture, a sequence of marks or sounds forming a logical picture, in understanding it as true or false. We explain the nature of a logical picture which is a proposition through a prior comprehension of 'true' and 'false'. A proposition is the kind of picture which represents reality and so is true or false.

But this, Wittgenstein now thinks, is a 'bad picture' (*PI* 136). This 'prior comprehension' of truth and falsity dissolves on reflection. To say that 'only a proposition can be true' is to say no more that that 'we predicate 'true' and 'false' of what we call a proposition' (*PI* 136). That is, 'true' and 'false' belong to our concept of a proposition but don't explain it. They are part of the use of the concept, and to see what they amount to we have to see what that use is. To say ' 'p' is true' is to say 'p', and ' 'p' is false' is to say 'not-p'. We only understand 'true' and 'false' if we first understand 'p', and then see what work additionally is done by the use of 'true' and 'false'. For example, to say "p' is true' is to stress that I am in a position to justify my asserting 'p', that I am confident in my assertion. Understanding 'true' is part of understanding the use of the proposition concerned, seeing what asserting p amounts to, what doubts and questions can arise in relation to it and in what contexts, how these are resolved, and so forth. What 'true' and 'false' amount to is seen in understanding the use, the life, of the proposition we are considering. They don't explain what a proposition is, rather they are explained (described) in describing the use of the proposition.

But how did we come to think that an abstracted sense of 'true' and 'false ' explained what a proposition is, that we had a prior understanding of them? In the *Tractatus*, the propositional sign is a picture of a possible situation, one which is true or false depending on the existence or otherwise of that situation. The propositional sign is a series of marks or sounds which is used to picture the situation. Starting from marks or sounds, we seem to need an explanation of how they come to do the work of a 'proposition'. It is only because we can see the situation in them, as we see the scene in the painted picture, that the marks can function as having a sense. And we explain what kind of picture it is by saying it is 'true' or 'false', it is a picture of 'reality', rather than of a fiction, say, or a day dream. We seem to need this apparatus because we start from the proposition as a 'dead' mark or sound, and then wonder how this is going to have the capacities of a proposition, something that says something meaningful about reality. The need for the conception of the 'logical picture', and then the explanation of what kind of picture the proposition is, one which is 'true' or 'false', derives from this starting point: looking at mere marks and sounds and wondering how they could come to be 'propositions'. So, although the *Tractatus* proposes that philosophical problems and resolutions misunderstand how logic is to be displayed through presuming an illusory 'external' position to logic and language, this same externality is present in developing the account of the proposition as a picture of reality. The notion of a proposition is not to be *explained*. Rather, 'Like everything metaphysical, the harmony between thought and reality is to be found in the grammar of language' (*PI* 255). We need to recognize that talk of 'marks' and 'sounds' in relation to language is an abstraction from its living application. We can, of course, perform that abstraction, but only because we begin from the language we speak and live in. In order to perform the abstraction, we must begin from the language in use, otherwise we have nothing to abstract from. And there, in language in use, the relation between what is said and what is the case is made in language itself. "An order orders its own execution'. So it knows its execution before it is even there?- But this was a grammatical proposition, and it says: if an order runs 'Do such-and-such' then *doing-such-and-such* is called 'executing the order"' (*PI* 458). And: 'It is in language that an expectation and its fulfillment makes contact' (*PI* 445). The point is simply that those words are only the order or the expression of an expectation if 'doing- such-and-such' or, say, 'his coming', are called 'executing the order' or 'the fulfillment of the expectation'. To suppose there is a problem here (how is it that 'when we say, mean, that such-and-such is the case, then, with what we mean, we do not stop anywhere short of the fact, but mean *such-and-such-is-thus-and-so*' (*PI* 95)?) is to suppose that the order or the expression of expectation are merely 'dead' marks or sounds, whose relation to future situations has somehow to be established. But as 'mere sounds or marks' they are not the order or the expression of expectation. No such question arises where there *is* the order or the expectation. The 'problem' of the 'harmony between thought and reality', to which 'picturing' is an answer, is the result of abstracting from living language, the product of adopting an 'external' viewpoint in which propositions, orders, expressions of expectations, are mere 'dead' signs, and we then have to conjure out of them a 'relation to reality'. This is, however, an illusion. The 'problem' cannot be formulated. As *PI* 120 notes 'When I talk about language (words, sentences, etc.) I must speak the language of everyday…your very questions were framed in this language-they had to be expressed in this language if there was anything to ask!' If we are to talk about an 'order', 'expression of expectation', 'proposition', we are not talking about marks or sounds, and their 'connection with reality' is simply that *this* is 'doing what is ordered', ' what is expected', 'what is the case'. The connection is made *in* language itself.

The 'picture' conception to explain the 'harmony between thought and reality' further involves the idea of our being able to 'read off' immediately the sense of the propositional signs, to grasp without mediation what the signs are a picture of. Explanation of meaning comes to an end and there we have to immediately grasp the relation of sign to reality, to see what the elementary proposition pictures. But how are we to understand this 'immediate grasp'? This 'problem' is one we express in language: that's where we got the notion of 'explanation of meaning' from. And as with 'the harmony between thought and reality', we find when we reflect on this 'immediate grasp' which *establishes* a relation between sign and reality, the notion dissolves and with it the problem. As 'explanation of meaning' is a term in everyday language, so the models for this are found there, 'ostensive definition', saying 'That's a red panda' and pointing, for example, or a verbal explanation, giving definitions, looking up in a dictionary, and so forth. The problem with both of these, if one tries to understand them as fundamental ways in which the connection between sign and reality is to be set up, is that they have their sense, and their capacity to explain meaning, only within contexts which presuppose that language is already up and running, a going concern. If we abstract from these contexts, to try to understand them as establishing a connection between sign and reality, we find ourselves unable to understand them as meaning anything at all.

An ostensive definition in everyday life presupposes a situation where the questioner has a particular problem ('What's that?' pointing at the red panda) which is only intelligible given that the questioner already has a familiarity with much of the situation with the exception, in particular, of what she is asking about. She is already able to identify other animals and other aspects of her environment at least to some degree. But if we abstract from any context, we find the notion of 'ostensive definition' disintegrates, it is no longer able to do what it achieves in everyday life, to explain meaning. For then the pointing and uttering a sound seems to be able to be understood in endless ways: is the pointing to the animal, the colour of the fur, to its shape, to the environment which lies over there, or maybe the pointing has to be understood in the opposite direction! How can the questioner latch on to what is pointed to? It seems then that the pointing is a 'dead sign' animated by my 'meaning' it, a mental act lying behind the pointing, which the questioner then has to somehow guess. 'But isn't it our *meaning* it that gives sense to the sentence? …And meaning something lies within the domain of the mind. But it is also something private! It is the intangible something, comparable only to consciousness itself' (*PI* 358), Wittgenstein ironically expresses the exasperation to which this line of thought leads. "Ostensive definition' suddenly seems impossible.

A similar fate envelops verbal explanations of meaning once we abstract them from the contexts in which in everyday life they are intelligible and do their work of explanation. As with ostensive definitions, giving such rules, verbal definitions and so on, presupposes a context within which there is a problem, an interruption in the otherwise unproblematic flow of meaningful life. If we abstract from any context, in order to understand rule giving as setting up the relation between 'sign and reality', then, once again, we seem to make 'giving a rule' impossible. To explain the meaning of a sign is to explain how it is to be used, applied, so that the grasp of the rule must determine its future application. But how can the rule I give do that? *PI* 188:'your idea was that this *meaning the order* had in its own way already taken all those steps. And it seemed as if they were in some *unique* way predetermined, anticipated- in the way that only meaning something could anticipate reality'. But, abstracted from any context, it appears the 'rule', this form of signs, could be interpreted in any way whatever. *PI* 198: 'But how can a rule teach me what I have to do at *this* point? After all, whatever I do can, on some interpretation, be made compatible with the rule'. And that applies equally to the giver of the rule as to the taker: we both of us have only the signs, so how are either of us to know how to apply them? How can the giving of the rule determine what 'I have to do at *this* point'? Rule giving as 'explanation of meaning' seems impossible. But, of course, these questions lack all purchase within the actual contexts within which explanations are asked for and rules, definitions, verbal explanations are given. There the verbal explanation is given in relation to a particular problem in the otherwise unproblematic flow of meaningful life and conversation. 'One might say: an explanation serves to remove or to prevent a misunderstanding- one, that is, that would arise if not for the explanation but not every misunderstanding I can imagine' (*PI* 87). There, the definition or rule is not a 'dead sign' awaiting interpretation by some mysterious act of 'meaning' which can somehow determine the endless possible applications of the word or words involved. As a 'dead sign', we think: the rule can be interpreted in any way, so no course of action could be determined by it. But then 'if every course of action can be brought into accord with the rule, then it can also be brought into conflict with it. So there would be neither accord nor conflict here' (*PI* 201). In depriving the rule of any context within which it can function, the notion of a rule disintegrates. But this shows, that in relation to rules (as we understand them in everyday language, and how else is this understanding to get off the ground?), 'that there is a way of grasping a rule which is *not* an interpretation, but which, from case to case of application, is exhibited in what we call 'following the rule' and 'going against it' (*PI* 201). What rule is at issue is shown *by* the application: that 1002, 1004 is a continuation of the rule '+2' is constitutive of the rule. The rule is explained by the application not the application by the rule. 'That's why 'following a rule' is a practice'(*PI* 202), the practice of its application. In learning, say, to add 2, one is being inducted into a practice of application which explains what rule we have to do with. As Wittgenstein remarks in *Zettel* 301: 'He must go on like this *without a reason*. ...And the *like this* (in 'go on like this') is signified by a number, a value. For at *this* level the expression of the rule is explained by the value, not the value by the rule'. This is why 'it's not possible to follow a rule 'privately'' (*PI* 202). The idea of a 'private language' disintegrates when one tries to articulate it. Such a language would be one which I alone can understand, which others could not learn. But if it is language, with words having meaning, then the meaning of those words lies in their application, in the practice of application. It is what is exhibited in what we call 'following the rule' and 'going against it' which shows what rule or word it is. Hence, for there to be a word there must be a practice of application, and so one shared or sharable. The notion of 'privately defining a word' which could not be understood by others, disintegrates: whatever is going on, it is not 'defining a word', and so not for the 'private linguist' either. These problems of the 'harmony of thought and reality' are the result of abstracting from the 'stream of thought and life' within which words have meaning (Z 173) so that language appears as a matter of 'dead' sounds or marks whose capacity to 'represent reality' now appears to require some kind of theoretical explanation. An abstraction from everyday life is, of course, in a certain sense a manifestation of the 'urge to understand the foundations'. Philosophical problems arise from it, however, where this abstraction is experienced as an *alienation*, where the abstraction appears to create an external position in terms of which we are no longer at home in language and we seem to have to justify to ourselves its capacity to say anything at all.

This alienation manifests itself similarly when the 'urge to understand the foundations' focuses on the forms of *accountability* which are intrinsic to our life in language, the ways we justify to others and to ourselves our thoughts and statements about our environments, the past, the feelings and sensations of others, and so on. When fundamental reflection is turned on these, they may appear problematic, unable to perform the role of accountability we, in everyday life, take for granted. If we justify our statements about the immediate past by appealing to memory, how can we know that a present memory accurately reflects a past event? If we justify our statement about the other's pain by referring to his cry, how can we know that the external sound indicates an 'internal' sensation? If we justify our statement that there is a squirrel in the tree by appealing to our just having seen it, how can we know that our seeing is adequate reason for claiming the existence of something beyond our consciousness? These 'problems' appear through 'analogies between the forms of expression in different regions of our language' (*PI* 90). 'I have a pain' looks like 'I have a coin in my pocket', only referring to an 'inner' event rather than to an externality. So 'he has a pain' looks like 'he has a coin in his pocket', but whereas I can know my coin and my pain, it looks like I can only know about his coin: the contents of his 'inner world' are essentially cut off from me. In order then to 'know' about his pains, I must construe statements about them in terms of what I can know, his external behaviour. Or again 'I remember putting my glasses down by the computer' sounds like 'I've a headache, probably through sitting too long at the computer'. It then seems possible to ask how this 'memory experience' can show me what happened before, and so we need some 'theory' to justify talk of the past, for example by construing all such statements as really about present 'inner processes'.

Wittgenstein doesn't want to replace these 'theories' with better ones, but to dissolve the appearance of there being a problem in the first place. We need to see that the analogies which impressed us are misleading and don't show us the real use of the relevant terms. 'But you surely can't deny that, for example, in remembering, an inner process takes place'- What gives the impression that we want to deny anything... The impression that we wanted to deny something arises from our setting our face against the picture of an 'inner process'. What we deny is that the picture of an inner process gives us the correct idea of the use of the word 'remember'. Indeed, we're saying that this picture, with its ramifications, stands in the way of our seeing the use of the word as it is' (*PI* 305). For "There has just taken place in me the mental process of remembering...' means nothing more than 'I have just remembered...'" (*PI* 306). And to see if I have remembered, no introspection is relevant: I need to see if my glasses are where I took them to be. Just as 'Meaning something is not a process which accompanies a word. For no *process* could have the consequences of meaning something' (*PPF* 291), so no process could have the consequences of remembering. When we do see 'the use of the word as it is', when we resituate it into the context of 'the stream of life' where it has its meaning, the problem of how an 'inner process' could do the work of remembering will 'completely disappear'.

The urge to 'understand the foundations' is an urge to understand ourselves, our human form of life in language. In this reflection, we, as it were, turn back on the 'stream of life and thought' to reflect on its 'possibility'. Philosophical problems emerge when this reflective movement becomes one of alienation from that stream. Then language appears as 'dead signs' requiring some explanation of how they can relate to and reveal reality, and the modes of justification we take for granted in our everyday lives appear unable to do their work. Alienated, we appear to occupy an external position to the stream of life and thought, having to justify to ourselves how language and accountability are possible at all. Wittgenstein works to relieve this apparent alienation by showing us that the urge to understand the foundations is to be satisfied by a reflective relation to the stream of life from *within*. The dissatisfactions with language and forms of accountability are shown to be illusory: they are expressed, as they must be, in our everyday language, and in terms of that the 'problems' can be dissolved, shown to only apparently make sense. We see, rather, the 'harmony between thought and reality' in language itself, in seeing the connections between a proposition, the questions and doubts that can arise in relation to it and how these may be resolved: in reminding ourselves of the role of the proposition in our lives. Similarly, the problems due to misleading analogies are to be relieved by showing how they are misleading and displaying the forms of justification in the stream of life, putting them back into their living contexts. Wittgenstein's strategy is to remove the sense of alienation which produces the problems and so bring us to a self-understanding of the flow of life and thought which constitutes us and our world, returning us to 'the spatial and temporal phenomenon of language' from the illusion of 'some non-spatial, atemporal non-entity' (*PI* 108 brf) we appear to occupy in alienation.

The 'urge to understand the foundations' is partly satisfied in reflection on the manifold and varied forms which accountability, giving reasons, takes. Doubt, questioning, giving reasons to oneself and others, are secondary phenomena, interruptions in the 'stream of life and thought', and so intelligible where something amiss in that normal flow can be indicated. The stream of life and thought is the 'ungrounded way of acting', a certainty, sureness of action which is not based on beliefs but rather forms the context within which we can have beliefs, questions, doubts and answers. Some quotations from *On Certainty* (trans. Denis Paul and G.E.M. Anscombe, Oxford, 1969) articulate this: 'The game of doubting presupposes certainty' (115); 'Giving grounds …comes to an end. But the end is not certain propositions striking us immediately as true, i.e. it is not a kind of *seeing* on our part; it is our *acting*, which lies at the bottom of the language-game' (204). 'Somewhere we must be finished with justification, and then there remains the proposition that *this* is how we calculate' (212), that is, *this* is what we call *calculating*; 'Doubt gradually loses its sense. This language-game just *is* like that.' (56). You walk through a wood at night: is that a person ahead or a tree stump? There's place for a question here because it is dark, one cannot see clearly. And it can be resolved by removing the obstacle, shining the torch. But in broad daylight, the 'doubt' loses its sense. If the question is to be intelligible, something further amiss needs to be indicated. I can doubt if I have two hands in certain circumstances: after an operation following a serious accident I could look to see. But here and now, the question has no intelligible place. I don't assure myself I have two hands by looking: why shouldn't I assure myself that there's nothing wrong with my vision by looking at my hands? But there is no place for assurance any more than there is for a question in normal circumstances. The normal flow of life and thought is the context within which specific doubts can arise, be investigated and resolved through looking, listening, touching, smelling. The normal stream of life is one within which we move, live, bodily in the world: we are always bodily with things and people in a *certainty, sureness of action.* When we are struck by this, what also strikes us is the *conditionedness* of these ungrounded ways of acting.

The possibility of these ungrounded ways of acting is conditioned in several ways. Induction into these forms of our life involves responding in the right way to training and the giving of examples. As Wittgenstein remarks in *Zettel* in respect of learning to calculate 'He must go on like this *without a reason* ...And the 'like this' (in 'go on like this') is signified by a number, a value. For at *this* level the expression of the rule is explained by the value, not the value by the rule' (301). 'For just where one says 'But don't you see...?' the rule is no use, it is what is explained, not what does the explaining' (302). Rules, definitions, ostensive or verbal, are secondary phenomena and have their intelligibility in terms of an already ongoing practice of using words 'without reason', as any reasoning, justification, appeals to the practice: that just is what 'adding 2' is, say. That we do catch on, continue the series in the normal way, respond appropriately to the particular examples, is a condition of there being such a practice and of our being able to participate in it. That this is so is one of the 'extremely general facts' (*PI* 142) involved in the possibility of our forms of language and life.

The normal flow of life may be interrupted by doubt and questioning and can be re-established in appropriate ways. Here the 'exception' is part of the expected course of events to be coped with in customary ways. But our normal practices would no longer be viable if we were faced by circumstances quite other than they are, where, as it were, exception became rule. 'The procedure of putting a lump of cheese on a balance and fixing the price by the turn of the scale would lose its point if it frequently happened that such lumps suddenly grew or shrank with no obvious cause' (*PI* 142). This reference to 'point' indicates, further, that, internal to our practices are

purposes and interests whose pursuit and engagement depends
on the holding of certain very general facts: that things do not
appear and disappear, grow and shrink without obvious cause,
for example. As Wittgenstein remarks in *On Certainty* 'Certain
events would put me into a position in which I could not go
on with the old language-game any further. In which I was
torn away from the *sureness* of the game. Indeed, doesn't it seem
obvious that the possibility of a language-game is conditioned
by certain facts?' (617). The holding of certain very general
facts makes possible the following of the purposes and interests
internal to the practices of the stream of our lives and whose
absence would remove the point of continuing with them.

At *PI* 327, Wittgenstein makes the striking claim 'If a lion could
talk, we wouldn't be able to understand it'. Of course, one
can cavil at this and ask how we could recognize it as talking
without being able to understand at least to a minimal degree.
But the point may rather be to emphasize the conditionedness
of *our* way of talking, that we can imagine forms of life being
very different. Our linguistic life depends on shared reactions
to the giving of examples so that we go on 'like this': such
reactions, we may surmise, may be very different with the
'lion' which would underlay concepts we could not acquire.
Further, 'Concepts lead us to make investigations. They are
the expression of our interest and direct our interest' (*PI* 570).
Concepts are part of practices and living practices embody
and develop interests and purposes. With different interests
one can imagine different practices, and again ones we may
only partially be able to enter into. A 'lion's' interest, although
partly understandable by analogy with some of our own, may
well extend beyond what we can share. A dog's very different
sense of smell means that its experience on a walk through the
countryside is very different from our own and undoubtedly
informs its activities in ways closed to us. They may well express
an interest, for example, in the pursuit of sensory experiences
beyond our capacities.

Further, what interests and purposes are significant for us and how they are developed may be conditioned by facts both biological and environmental. Clearly practices concerned with the maintenance and reproduction of life are central to human life. But how they are developed too will be conditioned by contingent factors. As David Cooper points out (in *Senses of Mystery*, Routledge, 2017, pp. 7-8)), conditions of scarcity mean that practices concerned with the maintenance of life will emphasize a concern with the capacity for control of relevant environmental factors. The development of natural science is an extension of such an interest. But if human life found itself in permanent summertime where the living was easy, where circumstances were always propitious, food and the essentials of life easily procurable, diseases unknown and accidental injuries rare, then developing practices concerned with the control of the environment would seem tangential to what really matters in life. The idea that such practices could show anything important about the world we live in would seem bizarre. Rather, we can surmise, practices which developed sensory appreciation of the environment and of ourselves, and ritual developments of recognition and celebration of the harmony of human life and the world would find obvious justification as revealing what is truly significant about humanity and its world.

In recalling this conditionedness, we realize that our forms of life and the reality they reveal could be otherwise. Imagine other reactions (the lion's), other general facts of nature (the constancy of things), other interests and concerns, other sensibilities and 'the formation of concepts different from the usual ones will become intelligible' (*PPF* 366). It is a vision that precludes our believing 'that certain concepts are absolutely the correct ones' (ibid.), that confronts us with the *givenness* of our life and the reality it reveals. By this I mean the following. The 'urge to understand the foundations' which prompts philosophical recollection is a mark of the *accountable* nature of human life (unlike that of animals). In following through this recollection, we arrive at ungrounded ways of *acting*.

Justification comes to an end and there we see what counts as 'justification' in this context. "Was I justified in drawing these consequences? What is *called* a justification here? Describe language-games' (*PI* 486). These practices are the context within which justification, accountability, takes place: they are not themselves accountable. They are 'ungrounded'. It is in terms of such practices that we see the 'harmony' between thought and reality, that we have a conception of the independently real that is at issue in justification. Human practices are practices of revealing 'the real', while what counts as the check of the independently real varies in systematic ways in different practices. These practices are a manifestation of, and express and develop, human interests, concerns and capacities. Our reflection then focuses on the conditionedness of these practices. Justification comes to an end in ungrounded practices, and their conditionedness shows us that this ungroundedness is not 'contact with reality as it any way is' ('our concepts are absolutely the correct ones'). We can conceive the absence of these human practices and the reality they reveal, as we can conceive other forms of life which reveal reality in ways closed to us (the 'lion', the dog on its walks). To speak of the 'givenness' of our life and the reality it reveals is to mark that we find ourselves in forms of life which are *authoritative* for us (are practices of accountability) but whose authority does not lie in that they reveal 'reality as it any way is' in terms of absolutely the right concepts. We find ourselves, then, *given* these practices and the reality they reveal. I use the term because it comes most naturally as an extension of ordinary usage, an extension which is required because we are driven here to speak of what underlies that usage. In the extension, there is no implication of a 'giver'. Indeed, there can be no explanation of this since any explanation must be in terms of practices internal to our life. To confront this is indeed 'to be struck by what, once seen, is most striking and most powerful' (*PI* 129). It is to confront the mystery of our life and its reality.

Rush Rhees in 'Wittgenstein's Builders' and in the collection of his working papers *Wittgenstein and the Possibility of Discourse* (Oxford, 1998) has stressed the limitations of the attempt to understand the relation of language to reality in terms of a variety of discrete language games. His fundamental objection is that it reduces learning to speak to the acquisition of a number of technical competences. 'But *do* the language games with the particular expressions show you the relation of words to things? ...Only on the assumption that they are *language* games ...Only because in this way you can learn to *talk* about things. Which is not the same as learning to go on with this game. If it stayed at that, you would not have learned to speak' (1998, p. 75). To learn to talk about things is to learn to engage in conversation and discussion, and this means to learn what is of interest, what matters: for example, to apply the grammar of talking about the past in relation to issues of human significance so that we can see the point of what is said. But further, to speak of these issues as of human *significance* marks the fact that language games are *lived* by human beings having *their* lives to live. Human beings do not just live but have their lives to live: life for the human being is an issue. Games are not part of a larger game, but language games are part of a language, and a language is language in the primary sense in being lived, as providing a way in which human beings can live (or fail to live) a *meaningful* life. Rhees comments 'unless there is meaning in life ...then nothing else that is said can be understood' (1998, p. 32). To find meaning in life is to see a unity in the various relationships, activities and concerns that constitute the substance of one's life. It is, in other words, to recognize a measure for one's life in terms of which that life can be seen by the individual *as* a whole. Human life, the life of language, one might say, contains a trajectory towards such a measure. The life of linguistic beings, which is *accountable* life, requires a measure for life as a whole.

What is the relation of Wittgenstein's practice of philosophical reflection to this issue? We have seen the earlier Wittgenstein draw a close connection between the dissolution of philosophical (logical) problems and that of the 'problem of the meaning of life'. There is only a 'problem' in the latter sense for one who fails to see 'the world aright', and so fails to see life aright, aspiring after an external measure in terms of which the world of facts can be judged, so that facts appear as 'good', 'bad', 'indifferent', and so on. The problem disappears when one realizes that the 'measure' lies internal to the structure of the world of facts, just as philosophical problems disappear when the internal logic of the world is allowed to show itself. The world of facts presupposes the 'I' which thinks. The world of facts is as it is, without discrimination, each fact, each proposition, having equal value with any other. The measure then lies in the 'I' living as itself, in terms of 'absolute value', so that what is willed is not dependent on outcomes in the world. The dissolution of philosophical problems leads us to see the world and life aright. Of course, individuals can live in terms of 'absolute value' and so see the world aright without philosophy, but philosophical reflection can remove, for those prone to fundamental intellectual reflection, obstacles to seeing how things really are.

But this whole vision is undermined in *PI*, revealed as a further manifestation of the 'external' viewpoint the *T* had thought to have banished with its distinction between showing and saying. The 'urge to understand the foundations' needs rather to find itself *in* the 'stream of life and thought' by being recalled ultimately to *ungrounded ways of acting, practices,* and through that to the *conditionedness* of our life in language. But does such a vision have 'existential consequences' in the way the Tractarian vision claimed? Does recovering the mystery provide a measure for life, dissolving the appearance of the 'problem', the 'issue' which human life is for itself? It certainly appears that *PI* rejects this possibility: 'Philosophy must not interfere in any way with the actual use of language, so it can in the end only describe it. For it cannot justify it either. It leaves everything as it is' (*PI* 124). But, of course, the *T* too had remarked that 'all the propositions of our everyday language, just as they stand, are in perfect logical order' (*T*5563) without that precluding the possibility, apparently, that certain widespread existential positions, both implicit and explicit in philosophical theorizing and ordinary life, were based on an illusion. We can, therefore, at least ask whether leaving 'everything as it is' might have consequences beyond the field of academic philosophy.

Wittgenstein certainly thought that certain intellectual practices in mathematical logic, psychology and psychoanalysis were the result of being 'charmed' by misleading analogies like those productive of philosophical problems and theories, so that if this were seen the charm would be dissipated and they would be seen in a different light. But more significant in this context are the misgivings Wittgenstein had about the publication of his work. In the Preface to *PI*, Wittgenstein writes: 'It is not impossible that it should fall to the lot of this work, in its poverty and in the darkness of this time, to bring light into one brain or another- but, of course, it is not likely' (p.4e). In a draft for the projected *Philosophical Remarks*(1930), Wittgenstein expressed similar doubts as to the possibility of a readership for his work. 'This book is written for those who are in sympathy with the spirit in which it is written. This is not, I believe, the spirit of the main current of European and American civilization' (*Culture and Value*, p. 6e). The 'spirit' of that civilization is 'Progress': 'Progress is its form rather than making progress being one of its features' (*CV* 7e). 'Typically it constructs. It is occupied with building an ever more complicated structure ' (ibid.) But he is 'not interested in constructing a building, so much as in having a perspicuous view of the foundations of possible buildings' (*CV* p. 7e). The 'urge to understand the foundations' is at odds with the spirit of the age. In so far as this urge finds some expression in contemporary philosophy, it is characterized by misunderstanding of what is really needed. It imitates science in the adoption of an illusory 'external' viewpoint and in the constant production of what Wittgenstein called 'philosophical journalism', endless 'research papers'. Rather, for Wittgenstein 'the place I really have to get to is the place I must already be at now' (*CV* p.7e). His later writings are directed to recalling us to the 'real foundations' and enabling us 'to be struck by what, once seen, is most striking and powerful'(*PI* 129). This is not a matter of a 'doctrine' or learning something new, but a recalling us to ourselves, to activate the 'urge' and then to intervene where we are misled by the temptation to ape science or by misleading analogies. 'I ought to be no more than a mirror, in which my reader can see his own thinking with all its deformities so that, helped in this way, he can put it right' (*CV* p. 18e). In this way, one can recover a sense for the 'givenness' of our human life in its fundamental forms and of the 'reality' they reveal. 'What has to be accepted- the given-is-one might say-*forms of life*' (*PI,* "Philosophy of Psychology: a Fragment" section 345). In doing this, one can re-establish the importance of those cultural forms which recognize, explore and celebrate this givenness: art, literature, music, religion, and so combat the pernicious influence of the worship of science in the civilization of 'progress'. 'People nowadays think that scientists exist to instruct them, poets, musicians, etc, to give them pleasure. The idea *that these have something to teach them*- that does not occur to them' *(*CVp. 36e). To bring us back to the 'place I must already be at now' and so to recall us to who we are, is, one might say, the project of Wittgenstein's work. And because of that he remarked 'I am by no means sure that I should prefer a continuation of my work by others to a change in the way people live which would make all these questions superfluous' (*CV* p.61e). That 'change' would be making central to human life a concern with its givenness and that of its world, and so creating a space within which art, religion and forms of spirituality can develop in shared forms. This was perhaps the limit to the existential implications of his work that Wittgenstein would have accepted, ridding ourselves of the illusions which prevented the recognition of the central importance to our self understanding of these forms of culture. Philosophers working in the spirit of Wittgenstein's work have tended to follow this line, seeing the 'issue' of the meaning of life as being addressed by a further language game, religion or related practices like magic in other cultures. (See, for example, Peter Winch,' Understanding a Primitive Society' in *Ethics and Action*, London,1972).

But does the recalling us to the mystery of our lives and world, which is I think the experience of engaging with the later Wittgenstein's writings, itself have existential implications in the sense that it provides a measure for life as a whole and thereby a basis for criticism of some of these cultural forms, even if this possibility is not developed in his thought?

Let me raise this question in relation to some of Wittgenstein's discussions of religion, fragmentary as they are. The philosophical problems with religion arise through 'misleading analogies', the product of forgetting the lived context of religious belief. Religious language looks similar to that used in speaking of people and their intentions and actions, of histories, and causal stories of natural events, but when construed in this way it appears to be seriously deficient. One can then either try to make up for these deficiencies by showing that the language is justified by appeal to some extra-religious standard or celebrate the deficiency as showing that religion is intellectually inadmissible. In relation to Christianity, the main focus of Wittgenstein's remarks in the *Lectures and Conversations on Aesthetics, Psychology and Religious Belief* (ed. Cyril Barrett, Oxford, 1967) and in *CV*, we appear to have an historical account of the birth, life and death of an individual, and yet what is said of this individual, that he is the Son of God, that he died for our sins, that he is resurrected, that he performed miracles, clearly goes beyond anything that could be supported by historical evidence. Indeed, it even seems historical evidence is shown to be inadequate in the account itself: the whole edifice of Christianity rests on four inconsistent narratives. No further evidence is sought as evidence for the events related even where this could be historically relevant, as would be a matter of course in relation to any other historical manuscript. Do Tacitus's references to Boudicca support belief in her existence given that we have no further textual or archaeological evidence? Such a natural question isn't raised in relation to Jesus within Christianity (although it obviously is raised by historians). The accounts given in the Gospels are not treated as we would treat any other historical documents. This narrative is embedded in a wider one of the creation of the world and human kind by God, the rebellion of humankind against God's will, and the final redemption of human sin by the death of Jesus and his resurrection. We appear to have the use of a name, God, used like that of a person, with reference to his actions and intentions (he creates, sees violations of his will, punishes, and so on), and yet an absence of much that normally goes with such a use. Does he exist, why does he do what he does, and how do we know about any of this? We appear to have a language which looks like that of historical narrative but where the appropriate language of belief, evidence, probabilities, and so on is missing. Given that the people who use this language also use that of ordinary historical narrative, perhaps this is not an indication of deficiency but rather that we have to do with another form of discourse entirely. As Wittgenstein points out, we learn the word 'God', but not in the way we learn the name of an aunt or of an historical figure like Napoleon. We're introduced to the aunt and examine evidence for Napoleon and his deeds, but nothing like this occurs with learning to use the word 'God'. Further, 'belief' here is used in an unusual way. 'One said, had to say, that one *believed* in the existence, and if one did not believe, this was regarded as something bad' (*LCAPR* p. 59). Or the believer believes in the Last Judgement. This sounds like belief in a future event (although it's 'at the end of time' so cannot be dated). But whereas for any ordinary prediction we would ask for evidence and we could have a range of positions from being certain, to being doubtful, saying 'well, possibly', to dismissal, in relation to such religious beliefs there is, as it were, only hot and cold, either affirmation or rejection. But the rejection isn't like that of some ill supported hypothesis nor is the affirmation like that of a well confirmed one. 'But he has what you might call an unshakeable belief. It will show, not by reasoning or by appeal to ordinary grounds for belief, but rather by regulating all in his life' (*LCAPR* pp53-4). And that is the point. We have what looks like an historical narrative but one whose acceptance has consequences no ordinary such narrative could have. You could believe some historical narrative (perhaps you saw a television programme about the life of Tutankhamun in which various experts assembled the evidence) but believing it may play no significant role in your life, and even if it did, that depends on your particular interests. But acceptance of the story of Jesus son of God is acceptance of what is to 'regulat(e) all in his life'. 'It strikes me that a religious belief could only be something like a passionate commitment to a frame of reference. Hence, although it's a belief, it is really a way of living, or a way of assessing life' (*CV* p. 64e). The religious story is the portrayal of a measure for life as a whole, for the whole of temporal existence. That is why it can't be justified since any such justification would appeal to some aspect of life itself (human reason, needs or whatever). 'Believing means submitting to an authority. Having once submitted, you can't then, without rebelling against it, first call it in question and then again find it acceptable' (*CV* p. 45e).

But what measure is this in the case of Christianity, Wittgenstein's central exemplar of religious belief? The story shows humankind rejecting God's will and living in terms of its own, so rejecting a measure for life as a whole in pursuing temporal goals, however 'lofty' these may be by human standards. 'Sin' is this rejection of God's will. Christ 's will is God's will, he is without sin, being both human and divine. To take this as the measure for life is to 'imitate Christ', to look towards willing 'for nothing', 'love', as the measure, and so embarking on 'dying to the world', to the temporal measures contained in human self assertion. The world in time is 'created' by God's will: that is, for 'nothing', out of 'love'.

We, in aspiring to live the life of divine love, to live for no temporal measure, imitate the divine giving of the world and life. 'Christianity is not a doctrine, not, I mean, a theory about what has happened and will happen to the human soul, but a description of something that actually takes place in human life. For 'consciousness of sin' is a real event, and so are despair and salvation through faith' (*CV*28e).

This is the context ('a way of assessing life') within which religious language is to be placed. When we do this, the philosophical problems dissolve. We see then that 'It doesn't rest on an historical basis in the sense that ordinary belief in historic facts could serve as a foundation …they are not treated as historical, empirical propositions' (*LCAPR*, p. 57). The issue of 'reasons for believing this story', which must, as with other historical narratives, lie outside the story, doesn't arise. Rather, the story is to give you reasons for living your life in this way. 'It would be as though someone were first to let me see the hopelessness of my situation and then show me the means of rescue until, of my own accord, or not at any rate led to it by my *instructor,* I ran to it and grasped it' (*CV* p. 64e).

But then, if it's not an 'historical account' in the sense of an account of what 'happened in time', does the believer not believe it recounts 'what happened'? Indeed, but we have to place 'happened' in the context within which religious language takes place, that of the entry into human life of the measure for the whole of that life. Such a measure has authority over life and so it comes, in that sense, from 'beyond' life- the manifestation within life of what commands with this total authority. Life changes in aspect, comes to be seen in a new way. In Christianity, we might say, it is the entry into life of the 'eternal' as the measure for life and for what occurs in time. 'Willing the eternal', turning away from the temporal as determining significance, is to imitate 'God's will' as the non-temporal giving of world and human life. It is this 'happening', the revelation of this measure in its binding, authoritative force, in which the believer believes. And this is beyond what we would call historical evidence. 'The historical accounts in the Gospels might, historically speaking, be demonstrably false and yet belief would lose nothing by this: *not*, however, because it concerns 'universal truths of reason'! Rather, because historical proof (the historical proof-game) is irrelevant to belief. This message (the Gospels) is seized on by men believingly (i.e. lovingly). *That* is the certainty characterizing this particular acceptance-as-true, not something *else*' (*CV* p. 32e). For if 'historically speaking' the Gospels were 'demonstrably false', *this* would be the way God manifested, by this fabrication: that would be the way the Eternal entered into the life of human kind as its measure.

This is *one* understanding of the 'givenness' of human life and the world revealed in it. In relation to the Abrahamic religions' understanding of the givenness of life and the world in terms of 'God's will', might we not ask, in the light of the notion of mystery uncovered in Wittgenstein's reflections, whether this is not in fact a move to 'explain' the 'giving' which that notion of mystery embodies? Do we need to understand the givenness of life and world by analogy to human action and intention, does this not involve an aspiration after an intelligibility of what must lie beyond understanding? Isn't it too close to conceptualizing what is beyond conceptualization, the givenness of our practices and what they reveal in their application? Doesn't the mystery to which Wittgenstein recalls us preclude appropriating this self-understanding in terms of such concepts? This question arises, not through seeing religion in inappropriate ways which seem to reveal its intellectual deficiency, but rather through contemplating what is shown when we attend to religious language in its living context. Of course, Christianity as a 'revealed' religion emphasizes precisely its going beyond anything that human reflective appropriation of their condition can arrive at, and indeed claims that only in such a 'going beyond' is it possible for the 'issue' which human life is for the individual can be answered, in 'revelation'. (I will look in greater detail at Kierkegaard's understanding of this in chapter 5 and the contrasting understandings of this 'issue' in Daoist and Zen texts). However, we can question whether this is so, whether being recalled to an experience of the mystery of our lives and the reality they reveal may not itself result in providing us with a 'measure' for life, so that Wittgenstein's reflective conception of philosophy might be seen as constituting itself a 'spiritual practice' among others. There is no evidence Wittgenstein himself shared such an understanding, but I now want to turn to a thinker whose thought in its mature form takes up the question of the existential implications of the revelation of the mystery of our lives and the reality they reveal, Martin Heidegger.

Chapter 2

*Heidegger: from authenticity
to releasement to the mystery.*

1.

Philosophical reflection arises out of our everyday lives: we in some sense understand ourselves, other people and what is other to ourselves prior to such reflection. How does philosophical reflection arise? Our everyday understanding incorporates, firstly, our concern with ourselves, with our own existence, not necessarily in a 'selfish' sense since altruism equally displays this concern, but in the sense that my life is *mine* to live. In having that concern, I have the concern to understand my self, my possibilities and capacities, and so what kind of being I am. The drive to philosophical understanding appears in the earlier Heidegger as a development of our everyday understanding of ourselves. As he wrote in 1922: the ' basic direction of philosophical questioning is not added on and attached externally to the questioned object-factical life- but is rather to be understood as the explicit grasping of a basic movement of factical life itself, which exists in such a way that in the concrete production of its Being, it is concerned with this Being' (*The Heidegger Reader*, ed. Gunter Figal, Bloomington, 2009 p. 41). Secondly, our everyday understanding is of living, in some sense, 'in the whole': we have an understanding of ourselves, other people and what is other to ourselves, and so of 'beings as a whole'. Our concern with our own nature is, then, at the same time, a concern with this 'as a whole'. There is, we might say, an implicit tendency towards questioning our own nature and the nature of the 'whole' in which we live. Philosophical questioning is raising this questioning to explicitness. In *Fundamental Concepts of Metaphysics* (hereafter FCM) Heidegger identifies the 'fundamental attunement 'of philosophy as 'homesickness' (p.9), a need to be at home everywhere …to be at once and at all times within the whole' (p.5). The questions which express this homesickness, 'what is my nature?' and 'what is the nature of the whole?', can be seen as developments of existing everyday life. The question of 'the meaning of Being' which is posed in *Being and Time* (trans. John Macquarrie and Edward Robinson, Oxford, 1967, hereafter BT) is the question of what makes possible this understanding of ourselves and 'beings as a whole'. Nevertheless, even if philosophical questioning can be seen as arising from tendencies in everyday life, it does not generally do so. That life is routinely unaffected by such questions. So what prompts their generation? We need to locate some experiences within the unreflective flow of life which can precipitate the move to philosophical questioning and understanding.

But before we address this, we need to note what is implied here for the character of philosophical understanding. We are ourselves involved in this understanding: it is a questioning of ourselves, an attempt at self-understanding. What is aimed at is self-transformation, a coming to know oneself, not a coming to know an object which stands over against us. Hence, the concepts developed through this questioning are not descriptive concepts of an object but, Heidegger says, are rather 'formal indicative'. They are formal in the sense that they will attempt to articulate the nature of our everyday understanding and what makes that possible, but 'indicative' since 'they can only address the challenge of transformation to us but cannot bring it about' (FCM p.296). They are concepts which are part of a self-transformative project, to come to a transparent understanding of ourselves which recognizes this as *self* understanding, one which must be taken on by the individual concerned and which will then inform their lives. In *BT* this transparency is achieved in 'authentic existence' and the aim of the work is to provide the opportunity for the reader to enter into such a transformative experience and live accordingly. But, of course, we are all such individuals, including the writer of *BT*. Ultimately the authority of the accounts which Heidegger produces lies in the agreement of its readers that they recognize themselves there.

The questions 'what is my nature?' and 'what is the nature of the whole within which I live?' can only arise if something like 'my nature' and 'the whole' can arise within everyday life and so then be subject to a reflection which is the progressive development of my concern with my life being my own. Heidegger sees them arising in *breaks* in the unreflective flow of everyday life in which 'the whole' and 'my nature' in a certain sense and to a certain degree manifest themselves. Our everyday life is an actualizing of certain possible human forms of life which initially we inherit and take over in the way that is accepted and current, as 'one' does, as Heidegger puts it. In living these ways of life we relate to other people and to things other than ourselves, both those which are made by us to further our ways of living and those we find already there around us. Human life is in this way an 'uncovering' of what is. The unreflective flow of this uncovering is subject to 'breaks' in which the *context* within which our life of concern is lived manifests itself. In certain breaks the 'whole' within which we live is to some extent revealed, in others the nature of our life 'as a whole' flashes up. Both provide the occasion for the further development of our concern to understand ourselves which manifests itself as philosophical reflection.

Such a break can occur with the absence of something we need for our activity or something becoming in some way unusable. Although such breaks are themselves routinely dealt with practically so life may resume its unreflective course, we replace the missing item or mend the unusable one, they can reflectively illuminate the context within which our unreflective life takes place. The break occurred because something was unusable or absent. This in itself points to the purposive nature of the stream of life, and so to the manifestation of things within it in terms of concern, of mattering in some way. And this directs us to the 'mineness' of the flow of life: it is always in the first person, it is *living* life, not life as a generalized abstraction or an object for an external reflection. We can reflectively realize here that our life is an issue for us, something we care about and so care about what we do and the things with which we have to do. We are addressing this issue in engaging with the purposive activity within which the break has occurred, in taking over certain historically given possibilities of human life, and so ultimately aiming at being a certain kind of person. Again, 'breaks' are exceptions, and this points us to the seamless nature of life. Things are not present as 'objects' as they may appear in such breaks. In 'our natural comportment towards things we never think a *single* thing, and whenever we seize upon it expressly for itself we are taking it *out* of a contexture to which it belongs in its real context: wall, room, surroundings' (*Basic Problems of Phenomenology,*, trans. A. Hofstadter, Bloomington, 1982, (hereafter *BPP)*, p. 162). This contexture Heidegger calls an 'equipmental whole', a contexture in which things are manifest in pointing to one another in purposive relations. 'Each piece of equipment is by its own nature equipment-for ...It is always... pointing to a for-which'(*BPP*, p. 163). Our relation to this whole is not one of relating to 'objects'': rather we *dwell* in it. It is a familiar context within which we live: things manifest themselves as they are *in* familiarity. Dwelling in a familiar context, things manifest themselves unobtrusively: ' Stairs, corridors, windows, chair or bench, blackboard, and much more are not given thematically. We say that an equipmental contexture environs us' (*BPP*, p. 163)). We dwell in such contextures in living a 'world', here we might say, 'the world of higher education'. The 'formal' characteristics of such environing worlds, 'worldhood', are what we understand in our unreflective life and which enable us to live 'in the whole'. It is in terms of this structure that we understand and relate to new situations involving beings we have not previously encountered. As Heidegger puts it, 'We always already understand world in holding ourselves in a contexture of functionality. We understand such matters as the in-order-to, the contexture of in-order-to and being-for, the contexture of significance. To exist is to cast forth a world in such a way that with the thrownness of this projection, with the factical existence of Dasein, extant entities are always already uncovered' (*BPP* pp 165, 168). We always dwell in such a contexture of significance, a world, within which things manifest themselves unobtrusively as we *live* the 'for which' which characterizes the world we are inhabiting. Things are manifest primordially unobtrusively in this seamless flow of purposive life, whether as 'equipment' or as pointing beyond to the wider context of teleological life: 'nature' is manifest 'as a being we come up against, to which we are delivered over, which on its own part already always is' (*BPP*, p. 169). 'Nature' does not appear here as an 'object', but rather in relation to purposive life. 'The wood is a forest of timber, the mountain a quarry of rock, the river is waterpower, the wind is 'wind-in-the-sails' (*BT, p. 100).* But through this relation, 'nature ' is revealed as the always already context of teleological life, and as such appears as 'the Nature which 'stirs and strives', which assails us and enthralls us as landscape' (*BT,* p. 100).

We are 'Dasein', 'there or here being', in living a form of life which uncovers beings *as* beings, we relate to them in terms of their nature. We uncover, say, hammers and nails as equipment, as 'ready-to-hand', in acting out our purposes. They are revealed in such 'circumspective concern' unobtrusively. In a break in this activity, they appear as 'present-at-hand', as obtrusively 'just there', as an object of examination and description. We are ourselves revealed, but as neither ready to hand nor present at hand but as 'existing', as taking over possibilities of life and so revealing other beings. In living these possibilities, I reveal other Daseins as existing beings. And this revelatory activity takes place against a wider humanly constructed and non-humanly formed background which can itself become the focus of our attention.

Breakdowns within practical activity provide the opening to reflection on the world lived by Dasein and so on worldhood which makes possible the uncovering of beings in their various possibilities of ready to hand, present at hand and existence. As our being is always an issue for us which we address by taking over possible ways to be, we are, as the 'there' within which beings can appear as beings, characterized by care. Beings are manifest to us as *mattering*, even if that is in a relation of indifference. Beings always appear through one or other of the various modalities of caring. Hence Dasein as 'being-in-the-world' is always 'mooded'. Mood as manifesting care is something we find ourselves in at any time, just as we find ourselves thrown into our being as Dasein and into the particular range of possible ways to be and our individual capacities for taking them over. Our being as Dasein is characterized by these form of 'thrownness', of what is constitutive of our being but in no way is the result of our activity. This is our 'finitude'. Initially, and for the most part, we inhabit this finitude implicitly without explicitly taking a stand in relation to it. The everyday Dasein, the default nature of the human being in relation to reality, is determined by the 'one' ('das Man'). Initially we take over possibilities of life and so of revealing beings by doing what 'one' does, and we continue in that way. Although this is a structural requirement of being a Dasein, or indeed of taking over new possibilities, living in terms of what 'one' does as characterizing a developed life is 'inauthenticity', allowing the 'one' to determine my life rather than myself, to live one's possibilities not as possibilities for me but as fixed and determined by the 'one'.

My relation to my finitude is constituted by mood, here in the complacency of living as 'one' does, an undisturbed sense of 'going with the flow'. This relation to my finitude can only be changed by mood itself and so is not something controlled by me. A 'break' can occur in the complacent unfolding of 'inauthentic' life within which the 'whole' of my life becomes available for reflective appropriation. In *BT*, anxiety, *Angst*, is the mood which descends revealing that I am not defined by the patterns of life I complacently live. The world I inhabit in terms of my conventional self loses meaning, loses its sense of mattering to me, revealing me as not at home, *'unheimlich'*, in the given world. This experience opens me to the possibility of living ways to be not as 'one' does but as mine. I am individuated, realizing that I have *my* life to live by fully confronting my mortality which marks out my life as mine. Fully facing this means recognizing that I have to explicitly take over possibilities in resolute choice, while recognizing at the same time that they cannot exhaust who I am. I must choose my 'hero', choose as my life one of the historical possibilities open to me by the 'there' of my Dasein. But it is always open to me to take on new possibilities and abandon old ones. In this way, according to *BT*, I take over my finitude. I am thrown into my mortal condition, my capacities, my historical situation of possible ways to be and my current life, which constitute my being as Dasein revealing beings. I take this over explicitly through making my thrown self my own, by resolutely choosing the self in terms of which I will address the issue of my being, choosing it 'for its own sake' and not for any further end. Out of anxiety, I am 'summoned' by the 'call of conscience' to take over my life as my own. Like the mood of anxiety, the call to authenticity is not something I do but something I respond to: it is my authentic self which calls me away from my conventional self.

Inauthenticity and authenticity are forms of existential temporality. Life is always in some form a taking over of the past, projecting into the future, and revealing the present. Inauthentically, living my life as 'one does', the past is determined and finished, the future is 'awaited' in terms of what happens which will determine who one is, while the present is that in which what happens to Dasein through its conventional behaviour occurs. Dasein understands itself here, Heidegger says, by way of things, its ability to be determined by success and failure. It thus 'expects' itself as what things give or refuse and so not in terms of Dasein's own self. The inauthentic present has priority as what happens determines the self I take myself to be. Authentically, however, the past is taken over as the source of possibility and so as never finished. I resolutely take over my 'situation', my finitude, in the present of decision in projecting myself towards death and so as a being who is never finished but always living as a self towards the end. The future of the living individuated Dasein is always open, never shut down by possibilities currently lived. It is this authentic future which has priority: in terms of it, the past appears as a source of possibiities some of which must be taken over in the present of decision. Authentically, Dasein lives its being as an issue so that its being can never be determined by what has been done or what has happened. Dasein is as living possibility. It is this which *BT*'s reflections direct us towards, pointing us to possible experiences within our own lives which can reveal the world and our life as a whole which may then precipitate a self transformation away from inauthentic to authentic life. We have to read these reflections as 'formally indicative', from out of our own concern with the issue which our lives are for us towards our own self transformation, not as some 'philosophical theory' to be pigeon-holed in a classificatory scheme of the 'history of philosophy'.

BT began by raising the question of the 'meaning of Being', that ultimately in terms of which we understand what is, being, in its various forms. The meaning of Being in this sense appears as time. Dasein is the there within which what is can be manifest as it is, as what it is and in its presencing. Dasein is living temporality, so that beings and their being are temporal too. The being of beings is characterized by *how* Dasein uncovers them, as readiness to hand in practical circumspection, as present at hand in the suspension of that circumspection, and as existentiality in living our lives as an issue and relating to other Daseins. These are the modes in which equipment, objects and Daseins can appear within the temporality of Dasein's 'there', the temporal space of first person life (that is, as lived and not as an object). The being of what is and of Dasein are to be understood on the basis of existential temporality. Time in that sense appears as the meaning of Being, the widest context within which 'what is' is understood.

Yet *BT* ends by raising this again as a question : 'Does *time* itself manifest itself as the horizon of *Being*?' (*BT* p. 488). The book as we have it is unfinished, a projected third division was to have announced a certain 'turn' in the inquiry which Heidegger at that time found no satisfactory way of articulating.

We can approach the issue addressed in this 'turn' by reflecting on the 'uncovering' of what is which characterizes Dasein as the 'there' within which beings can manifest themselves. We've seen that when reflection takes place out of breaks in everyday comportment, life is revealed as uncovering of beings, of what is, as equipment, objects and Dasein itself. Such 'uncovering' may involve the use of statements, 'The picture is askew', say. We say such a statement is 'true' or 'false'. But to say it's true is simply to say it uncovers the picture, while thematizing its askewness. The statement does the same thing, at one remove, as the experience of turning around and looking at it. The true statement may be said to 'correspond with the way things are', but this has to be understood in the sense that this mode of human comportment, asserting, is a form of uncovering beings, which is the nature of human comportment in general. We turn around and say 'Yes, that's right', that is, the assertion uncovered what the experience does. Experience and asserting as forms of uncovering depend on the prior uncovering of world. I can make assertions and have experiences of beings only because I inhabit a world. I can explicitly notice beings in assertions or experiences only because I am uncovering them in the flow of my everyday life immersed in the worlds I inhabit. But such uncovering of worlds and so my nature as the 'there' within which beings can be uncovered must themselves be *given*. We find ourselves 'thrown' into our being as being-in-the-world. Uncovering, unconcealment in this fundamental form underlies the other possibilities of unconcealment, of uncovering. The fundamental form of unconcealment is the very giving of the human as being-in-the-world, a giving which proceeds from essential mystery. Recognizing this would be the recognition of our fundamental finitude, and fully recognizing it would be to live finitely.

The issues which provoke the 'turn' are indeed present in Heidegger's thought at the time of *BT*. We can identify at least three such concerns. 1) In *FCM*, a lecture series contemporary with *BT*, Heidegger writes 'Finitude is our fundamental way of being and is truly in becoming finite' (p.6), and connects this with the giving of our nature as the there for the manifestation of what is: 'When we ask about the essence of man we are asking about ourselves, concerning a *being which it is given over to us ourselves to be*. Being delivered over to Dasein in this way is the index of an intrinsic finitude' (p. 281). Further, this givenness of our 'essence' is here expressed in terms of mystery: 'The mystery is lacking in our Dasein', ' we must concern ourselves with preparing the possibility within which something like a mystery of this Dasein could once again be encountered '(pp. 164, 172). Fundamental to the notion of our finitude here is the givenness of our nature as Being-in-the-world, as the there within which beings can presence. How is this givenness to be thought and related to? Is it sufficient to suggest, as *BT*'s 'authenticity' seems to, that 'resolute choice' is adequate to 'becoming finite'? If our being as Being-in-the-world is given, and all thought and decision takes place within the world Dasein lives, then that givenness must appear as proceeding in some sense from 'beyond' being-in-the-world, and so 'beyond' the articulation of anything occurring within the world, and so out of 'mystery'. Or rather, out of *the* mystery, since this is not a mystery which can be resolved into transparency. Transparency, rather, is recognizing it as the mystery. A relation to this surely cannot be understood in terms of the resolute choice of possibilities occurring within the given world. How can we speak of this mystery, what is an appropriate relation to 'it'? Must then 'becoming finite' take on a very different sense than that we find in *BT*?

2) This is related to the further issue of how the notion of 'what is', of 'beings', is understood in *BT*. Beings are uncovered by Dasein in living ways to be. As such, beings are uncovered as equipment, objects or as Daseins, as ready-to-hand, present-at-hand or as existence. They are uncovered in modes of Dasein's being: in circumspect activity, the suspension of that activity, or in inauthentic or authentic concern with one's own or others' Dasein. Yet what is uncovered is *beings, what is*, that is, a measure for human activity, thought and speech. Our thoughts or utterances can be true or false, reasonable or unreasonable, and our actions appropriate or not, skilful or not, and so on, all with reference to 'what is' as the standard or measure. But what is the nature of this *claim* on us, the *authority* which what is has for us?

The meaning of being we are told is time understood in terms of Dasein's temporality: what is presences within the temporality of Dasein's finite existence. But what is *presences*, has authority for us, claims us, and this is essential to the meaning of being. How is this authority to be understood? How is temporality to be understood in terms of this authority? Perhaps authority derives from the mystery of the givenness of our Being-in-the-world, and that givenness, as what is 'always already' in living temporality points towards another sense of time. These issues are again pointed to in *FCM* but not directly addressed: world projection 'is *that* occurrence that lets the *binding character* of things spring forth as such' (p. 363). How this is so remains a question.

3) *FCM* has said that 'The mystery is lacking in our Dasein' (ibid.). The lecture course discusses at length a fundamental disposition, profound boredom, which, like anxiety, reveals Dasein's relation to world as a whole and so to beings as such. But it is not presented, as anxiety perhaps is in *BT*, as some timeless possibility for Dasein, but rather as something which may characterize our Dasein now, whether we know it or not (and it is rather the latter which is the case). Is it ultimately boring for the Dasein in contemporary man as such? Heidegger asks (p.12). The fundamental emptiness that bores us 'is rather attested by the very activities with which we busy ourselves in our contemporary restlessness' (p.164). Here the fundamental attunement reveals an historically specific mode of Being-in-the-world and of the world it inhabits. This suggests that the unity of 'the whole' we inhabit is itself historical. In *BT*, the wholeness of Dasein's existence and so of the world Dasein projects is formed through authentic choice. But this cannot address the restriction on the historically available ways to be which appear for resolute choice. We cannot choose to be a samurai warrior or chivalric knight. There is in this sense a 'whole' of possible ways to be which is historically situated. What is the nature of this 'wholeness', and how is this related to the claim of what is which can be uncovered in living historically specific forms of life? These questions reflect back on how we understand philosophical questioning. In *BT* it appears as a development of

a fundamental trajectory of everyday life, taking over my life as mine and so raising the issue of the nature of my existence and of the world I inhabit. Its origin, we might say, lies internal to life, although it involves what is not my doing, the happening of anxiety and breaks in my engagement with the world. Yet philosophical reflection is not a constant feature of human life. Humans lived for millennia without this specific human possibility manifesting itself. How do we understand the nature of its emergence in the West with the Greeks? And how is that emergence related to the historically specific possibilities of life we inhabit now?

Addressing these questions requires a 'turn' in reflection, from one within Dasein's existence to one on the givenness of that nature itself. And that will transform how we can live this deepened understanding of our 'finitude': no longer by resolute choice in taking over our historically given possibilities, but rather in entering into a relation to the mystery of the givenness of our nature and our world.

2.

For Heidegger, both early and late, 'philosophy' is a thinking of the 'whole' within which we live and of which we are a part. He was concerned to show throughout his career that this thinking must arise out of the everyday way we are in the world, in a reflexive recognition that this 'factical life' is the primordial way in which reality, both of ourselves and of what is other to us, manifests itself. In this reflexive movement, we come to see life and ourselves in a new way which requires, if we are to avoid self-deception, a self-transformation. This new way is, then, a form of self-knowledge, an uncovering of what had been concealed in living prior to reflection. The concepts developed in this inquiry are therefore produced within this context, as proposals for self-recognition on the part of the reader which may open them to the possibility of a self-transformation. As we've seen, the earlier writings call such concepts 'formal indicative' to recognize this, and although this terminology is absent later on, the context of self-understanding and self-transformation is not. The later writings try to open us to the possibility of an 'experience' of Appropriation, of the 'it gives' of the belonging together of our lives and the manifestation of reality, which in turn opens us to the possibility of 'dwelling', of living in such a way that the revelation of what is, both of ourselves and what is other to us, points to the mystery of the giving. In this way, the writings both early and late, arise out of and address us in terms of the concern we have with our own lives, appealing to us to recognize ourselves in what they say and to live in terms of the new vision they offer of ourselves and our world.

This thinking, directed towards an explicit understanding of 'the whole' which we implicitly recognize in living our lives, is a continuation and disruption of the tradition of such explicit thought of the 'whole' which constitutes Western philosophy. It is a continuation in the sense that it takes over the directive to such explicit thinking of the whole, but is disruptive in its determination to get us to recognize that this thinking must, in arising out of everyday life, recognize the primordiality of that life in understanding the whole. 'Reality' is to be understood through a reflexive movement which brings out what is concealed in our unreflective understanding.

The earlier writings appear to open up the question of 'the whole' in a direct appeal to the reader. The notions of the 'whole' and of the nature of the human being are shown to arise from within our factical life through experiences of breakdown in its smooth unreflective flow. Breaks in the course of circumspective concern open up the 'world' of our engagements and so reveal 'worldhood', that which makes possible living within any particular world. The experience of angst is a breakdown in the smooth run of our relation to the forms of life lived within these worlds, revealing we are other than those forms and so opening us to the question what form our relation to them should take to recognize this otherness. These writings appear to address us simply as human beings, appealing to universally significant experiences and their unveiling of universally valid insights into our condition. The later writings, on the other hand, situate themselves in a culturally distinct history, addressing us in terms of an interpretation of our situation in respect of how the 'whole' manifests itself now as the latest development of a tradition. The reason for this change appears to be something like this. The reflections in the earlier writings on 'the whole', 'beings as such and as a whole', are responding to a demand to think this explicitly. Such a demand and the possibility of responding to it depend for us on there being a tradition of such explicit thinking. (We are not in the position of the early Greek thinkers at the inception of this tradition). These reflections are made possible by what has come before and the problems that has thrown up. The earlier writings see something radically amiss with the tradition: that it did not focus on the primordial way reality manifests itself and so failed to allow the philosophical reflection to arise from it. In this way, it proceeded out of an 'oblivion of Being': it thought the nature of beings in neglect of the living context which allowed beings to be manifest in the first place. But since all thinking takes place in terms of a tradition, in order to rethink it, we need to uncover what made that tradition possible, something which it presupposed but was unthought: unconcealing itself, the condition for the unconcealed which is the focus of the tradition. In actualizing this possibility, in bringing unconcealing to language, we can then readdress the issue of that tradition, the explicit thinking of 'the whole', and develop an appropriate language to respond to the issue in a new way. Heidegger asks:'is there a *first* possibility for thinking, …a possibility from which the thinking of philosophy would have to start out, but which as philosophy it could nevertheless not experience and adopt?' Heidegger's later thought 'only attempts to say something to the present which was already said a long time ago precisely at the beginning of philosophy and for that beginning, but has not been explicitly thought' (*The End of Philosophy*, trans. J. Stambaugh, London 1973, pp. 59,61). How, then, does Heidegger understand the inception of the tradition of explicitly thinking 'the whole' in European thought and life?

Heidegger now calls the advent of such fundamental reflection a 'happening' and the inception of 'historical existence'. 'Historical existence' in this sense is existence lived in terms of a self-understanding informed by an explicit understanding of the 'whole' within which and of which Dasein lives. We've seen that Heidegger's reflections occasioning 'the turn' reveal the ultimate 'unconcealing' as the very giving of the human being as the there within which what is can presence. Now the focus is on this givenness, Heidegger refers to our human being as the 'clearing' within which beings can presence rather than as Dasein, a term which emphasized our active role in uncovering what is. He now sees the inception of 'historical' Western humanity, of living within an explicit understanding of human and non-human reality in their unity, as lying in the initial conceptualization of this 'clearing' in early Greek thinking.

This occurs as a response to the fundamental disposition of *wonder*. Wonder is a fundamental break in the flow of unreflective purposive life which *happens* to the human being and in which, as with the 'breaks' in *BT*, a revelation of one's situation is glimpsed and so open to expression and articulation. This happening is, then, an 'unconcealment' of what is concealed in unreflective life, its 'nature'. In this unconcealment, the familiar world appears stripped of its familiarity. 'In wonder what is most usual itself becomes the most unusual ...In wonder, what is most usual of all and in all, that is *everything*, becomes the most unusual' (*Basic Questions of Philosophy*, Bloomington, 1994, p. 144). In wonder, what is encountered in familiar life is revealed as *physis*. Physis 'means the emergent self-uprising, the self-unfolding that abides in itself... This sway is the overwhelming coming-to-presence that has not yet been surmounted in thinking, and within which *that which* comes to presence essentially unfolds as beings. But this sway first steps forth from concealment- that is, in Greek, *aletheia* happens- in so far as the sway struggles itself forth as a world. Through world, beings first come into being.' (*IM*, p. 64) What is glimpsed in the break of wonder is the 'binding character of things' (*FCM* p. 363),of 'beings' as claiming us, as having authority for us in being unconcealed in the living of the purposive practices which constitute our world.

Human life is revealed as uncovering beings, what is, and this, not as something we do so that we could be understood in distinction from it, but as what we *are*. Human being 'was determined as that being whose distinctivesess consists in perceiving beings as such' (*BQ*, p. 121). Life is a constant unconcealing of beings which emerge of themselves in that activity and so always in relation to concealment, to mystery. In phusis, beings are uncovered and so 'where this happens Apprehension (noein) holds sway ...as belonging to Being' (*IM* p. 147). 'If human beings have a part in the happening of this appearing and apprehension, then they must themselves be, they must belong to Being ...apprehension is a happening in which humanity itself happens and in which humanity ...itself comes to Being' (IM p. 150). Phusis is the constant unconcealing of what is in which humanity is unconcealed as revealing beings. Phusis 'means this whole prevailing that prevails through man himself, a prevailing that he does not have power over, but which precisely prevails through and around him' (FCM p.26). Here we and our familiar world are revealed explicitly in terms of their 'reality'. We are as revealers of what is: our nature is to be claimed by what manifests itself in the flow of our purposive lives, and this nature has itself the character of a claim. It is something we must take on, it is something we can live more or less well, and so its claim is that of standards both in the revelation of what is and of ourselves. In this transformation, the flow of our familiar life is revealed as the constant unconcealing of what is which emerges of itself (and its concealing, in that both we may succumb to mere seeming, deception, and so on, and in that any unconcealment always reveals further concealment). There is no unconcealment without concealment, so there is no telos of total illumination towards which this is directed. There is only phusis, the constant upsurge of what is in the flow of human life. The fundamental disposition of wonder is itself a mysterious upsurge into human life. It is beyond all explanation as any explanation only occurs within the world which is 'opened up', understood in terms of 'being'. In terms of this understanding, the human being is summoned to preserve the relation to concealment which the recognition of *physis* involves, and so to 'set Being to work and thus hold open beings as a whole' (*IM*, p.174). Beings appear as beings in standing out from the familiar, the taken for granted. This vision underlies the agonistic understanding of human life in which 'struggle first projects and develops the unheard, the hitherto unsaid and unthought' (**IM** p.66). This refers first to the capturing of the experience of concealment and the self emergent nature of reality in early Greek thought and then to the living of this vision in action and creation, in the constant drive to surpass what has been, thus revealing the familiar as familiar.

Heidegger's account of Early Greek thinking is informed by the same concerns as that evident in the earlier texts. Philosophical reflection emerges out of unreflective life, and it is central to maintain this sense of a *living* problem. An experience, not something which is of the thinker's doing, precipitates a break in unreflective life which opens up a vista on familiar life which enables reflective appropriation. The thinker is *involved* and *implicated* in this reflection. It concerns the thinker as it is a reflection on their own being, a form of fundamental self-understanding. And it is a reflection on familiar life which includes the thinker: it is a reflection on 'the whole', beings (including the thinker) 'as such and as a whole'. Hence the nature of the reflective account is not a description of some 'object' which is conceptually and existentially distinct from the thinker: it is a self-reflection which nevertheless claims a validity for any other 'I' who engages in it (or at least any other 'I' who lives in the same familiar world as the thinker). The account invites the reader to acknowledge the description as true for them, to take it on, not merely intellectually, but in its existential consequences. In *BT,* the break of anxiety in the individual's relation to the forms of life they live reveals their freedom and the necessity of taking over their lives as their own in resolute choice, just as the breaks in circumspective concern reveal the nature of the world within which that life is lived. So now for the Greeks, wonder disrupts the flow of everyday life revealing it as the uncovering of what is as *unfamiliar,* in its claim on us, and so as emergent out of concealment. Just as BT's reflection resulted in the existential requirement of authentic choice, so this new vision of life, bringing out what was concealed in our immersive life, contains its own requirement: to preserve in living forms of life a relation to concealment.

This, then, is a reflection which proceeds out of living experience and so recognizes it as a reflexive form of self-understanding and self-appropriation. Just as the earlier writings, as 'formally indicative' discourse, invite the reader to recognize themselves in the accounts and to take on existentially their consequences, so the form of the writings of the early Greek thinkers has a parallel nature. Theirs is not a 'theoretical' account to be read in a disinterested spirit, but one to be appropriated out of a concern with one's own life and world. Their fragmentary aphoristic form disrupts the familiar flow of pragmatic and descriptive discourse to provoke the experience of wonder and so open up the vista within which the vision of life as the revelation of what is as phusis can take hold.

Although the Greeks experienced what is as unconcealed in the flow of purposive life and so in relation to concealment, they did not explicitly think what made this experience possible. 'For the Greeks unconcealedness remained unquestioned' (*BQ* p.115). 'For them, it is beings seen in terms of the field of view of unconcealment that is the focus of attention. The task was to apprehend beings as beings and the determination of man as that being which in the midst of beings lets beings hold sway in their unconcealedness' (*BQ* p.128). They did not think the nature of unconcealment, but rather concerned themselves with how things and themselves looked in its light, namely as other to their familiar grasp. It was a reflective experience of their familiar world and of themselves in terms of unconcealing, so that they and the beings that are present to them are experienced in relation to concealment. Their focus was, according to Heidegger, on how beings and themselves appeared in their otherness in this experience, and so on the claim made on them by the relation to concealment. But what made this experience of themselves and beings as other possible is not thought. That is, the giving of human life as the clearing within which what is can appear, be present, unconcealment in its fundamental form, is not thought. This concealment of the nature of unconcealment in the inception is what Heidegger calls 'the oblivion of Being'. That inception thought the 'whole' in terms of this experience of unconcealment, that beings are revealed as self emerging, of the manifestation of the otherness of the familiar world, but precisely because it did not address what made that experience possible it could not think the 'whole' adequately. The tradition of thinking the 'whole' explicitly in its 'opening' begins with this focus on beings, on the unconcealed, rather than on what allows the unconcealed to appear as such. Beginning with the 'oblivion of Being', Heidegger calls this tradition the 'History of Being', the 'epochs' of this history being, not so much periods of time, but ways in which what was concealed at the inception retreats ever more surely. 'Epochs' here refers to the Greek 'epoche', withdrawal.

The tradition of understanding the human and the world in an explicit conception of their reality is the result of trying to think the 'whole' through a focus on beings, the unconcealed. The early Greeks experienced beings as unconcealed in the living of everyday life, and experienced that life as a claim to preserve their otherness, their nature as self manifesting, as *physis*. But in the immediate aftermath of the inception, the unconcealed is no longer understood in its unconcealedness, as having an essential relation to concealment, as emerging in the living of the forms of life which constitute our world, but rather as what is already there to be understood and grasped as a 'whole'. 'By disavowing itself in and for forgotteness, the mystery leaves historical man in the sphere of what is readily available to him and leaves him to his own resources' ('The Essence of Truth', in *Martin Heidegger: Basic writings*, ed. D. Krell, London 1978, (hereafter *BW*), p. 134). Beings are no longer experienced in terms of arising in everyday life, but rather, in the language of BT, as 'present at hand', that is, how they are manifest when the flow of life is interrupted and they are available for description, as objects for our representation. The interruption now, in terms of the project of thinking 'the whole', is of the flow of life itself, so that what emerges there now becomes alien to it, presenting the problem of how we can again be united with it. The task is then first to grasp beings as thinkable, but now in terms of a standard separate from familiar life. Our everyday forms of life no longer reveal what is as it is but have a contact with reality only in pointing towards a 'reality' beyond them. Everyday temporal life and its world are subordinated to a 'higher' reality. It becomes something to be grasped in terms of that higher conception. The concealment of the mystery which underlay the revelation of the otherness of the familiar as its 'being' is now intensified, as relating to the 'whole' becomes a *project* of making that whole 'present', graspable in thought, and so progressively eliminating the sense of mystery which attended the initial manifestation of the otherness of what is. This development, like the occasioning of wonder and the manifestation of otherness itself, is not a human doing but an intensified concealment of concealment that comes upon the Greeks. The familiar world, including ourselves, appears no longer as other but as masterable in terms of some further conception of 'reality'. It is this project of grasping 'the whole' and so mastering it in thought that unfolds as the 'history of Being'. As Heidegger says in' The Essence of Truth',this leaves humanity to replenish 'its 'world' on the basis of the latest needs and aims, and fills out that world by means of proposing and planning. From there man takes his standards, forgetting beings as a whole. He persists in this, and continuously supplies himself with new standards, yet without considering either the ground for taking up standards or the essence of what gives the standard. In spite of his advance to new standards and goals, man goes wrong as regards the genuineness of his standards. He is all the more mistaken the more exclusively he takes himself as subject, to be the standard for all beings ...((But even here)) the mystery holds sway, that is the forgotten and hence 'inessential' essence of truth' (ET pp134-5).

This passage clearly indicates the trajectory of Heidegger's later thought. The appearance of unconcealment to the Greeks opened up the explicit taking over of 'living in the whole' rather than living it immersively. Such explicit taking over initially was in terms of the manifestation of the familiar world as unconcealed, and so as other, and it is this essential relation to mystery that gives the binding force to the 'standards' which then informed Greek life, of preserving the otherness of the familiar world and life. Only a relation to mystery gives binding force to standards. As Heidegger later put it in the' Letter on Humanism' :'Only in so far as man, ek-sisting into the truth of Being, belongs to Being can there come from Being itself the assignment of those directions that must become law and rule for man ...Otherwise all law remains something fabricated by human reason' (*BW*, pp 238-9). Western humanity, precipitated upon the necessity of explicitly understanding themselves and the whole within which they live, progressively moves further away from the concealment, the mystery, which underlay the initial manifestation of this need. It embarked on the project of *grasping* the whole, of making it present. Each attempt at thinking the whole in this way necessarily fails since it cannot address the mystery of the givenness of Dasein as the clearing of what is within which this very process of attempting to make present takes place. The binding force of standards which emerges from this process of world understanding derives not from the sources of authority projected in them (which are human projections attempting to deal with the issue of making the whole 'present') but from the concealed relation to concealment itself, the very givenness of life and world which these projections unknowingly respond to.

After the Greek inception, 'beings as beings' becomes, not the revelation of the otherness of the familiar world which tears the human out of the security of the everyday, but something to be grasped by the thinker who now stands, not claimed by beings in transforming the one who is addressed, but over against them, as what is to be understood 'as a whole'. With the concealment of this otherness and its claim, 'reality' initially becomes an intelligible structure, the Forms or Ideas which provide the *telos*, the end, for all temporal beings which can be grasped by us in *theoria*, contemplation.

Plato and Aristotle articulate and sketch out a new way to be human and a new form of the real. The source of the bindingness of our ways of thought and action lies in the Forms or Ideas which are fully intelligible, fully illuminated and which are permanently present. They are therefore not subject to change. This permanent standard of intelligibility is the measure of the reality of what is. The Forms, the *logos* of the *kosmos*, are what is fully real. The things of our world, the world of change, and we ourselves, lack full reality. They are real either as imitating the Forms in changeable and ultimately unintelligible matter, or, with Aristotle, in pointing in their characteristic forms of being towards the unchangeable as their *telos*. Human life, in so far as it is in contact with reality, is characterized by the primacy of intellect which can apprehend the unchanging intelligible measure for what is, and so the appropriate form of life for such a being is *theoria*, contemplation of that measure. The real as unchangeable and intelligible has ultimate authority over human life and thought, and so there is a final truth about human life and the *kosmos*, although this involves reference to a fundamental unintelligibility which is the ultimate cause of the contingency of our lives and of what we encounter within them. And this, in terms of the (unrecognized) project of making the 'whole' present, is a problem, a provocation to further interpretation.

When Christian experience became conceptualized in terms of the resources of Greek philosophy in Christian theology, the source of the authority of our ways of life and thought lies in the Creator God. For God, there is no mystery in the entirety of the temporal world: all is understood in terms of the complete illumination of the Greek Forms. The forms become ideas in the mind of God which give rise to creation *ab nihilo*, entirely the result of divine action. Man is given reason which can perceive the necessity of the Divine creator and so is able to understand the way all things in their characteristic ways of being point to Him as their end, their *telos*. But this gives only partial illumination to the world and to life. There is mystery for us, concealment, but only because of our fallen finite nature. Through faith we can believe in the full illumination of God's presence and that we are promised to enter into that presence after death. The appropriate form of human life is an orientation towards salvation, counting the obstacles and misfortunes of life as indications of our dependency on God, as God given and so to be borne in the expectation of eternal life. The authority of God is dominion over the world which is His creation. Again, in terms of the concealed project of making the 'whole' 'present', the 'mystery for us' of this vision is a further provocation to interpretation.

The Medieval world withdraws before the emergence of a new form of human life and of the understanding of reality. Here the total illumination of God's vision is transferred 'in principle' to the human. This again is a result of the underlying trajectory of world understanding, the hidden project of relating to the 'whole' in terms of 'presence', excluding mystery, concealment, from the sense which 'reality' has. What is, and human life itself, is now 'in principle' fully intelligible for us, although, of course, at any time, much remains beyond us. But what is beyond us now is nevertheless understandable, even if in striving towards that understanding new realms of ignorance will be revealed. Man can understand reality because the real is what can be subsumed under universal law, and man attains autonomy by giving himself law in morality, politics and social life. The source of the bindingness of the real lies, therefore, in Reason. We live in a rational world, one conformable to our reason, although our grasp of it is incomplete. Nevertheless, there is a final truth towards which our efforts at understanding are directed. The appropriate form of life for the human is the autonomous life of reason which can give us both self-mastery and mastery of the world. What is has essentially the form of an object for the autonomous subject. The obstacles and misfortunes of life are no longer reminders of our God dependency but provocations to further understanding and control.

For Heidegger, this Modern dispensation has now undergone a mutation, where the notion of the real as 'object', and so representable in a complete way, has given way to that of resource, *Bestand*, for human remaking. Here the unifying principle of the 'world' of the contemporary human is no longer Reason but will.

The real is understood as such when it can be construed in such a way that it is 'on hand' for the projections of human will. But human will is not directed towards some final goal, as salvation had been for the Medieval understanding and the perfection of rational life for the Modern. It rather has the character of the 'will to will', the constant self-overcoming of whatever has already been made. The very notion of 'givenness' is a provocation to overcoming. It is as if life becomes motivated by a dream of the absence of all resistance to the free flow of the will in endlessly recreating the world and human life. (That this should lead to the dream of overcoming the human itself through creating artificial forms of life for which we may become mere resource seems only taking this to its conclusion). Modernity's conception of a final truth, of the intelligibility and representability of reality for humanity is replaced by an overcoming of all finality: the world and humanity appear endlessly reformulable. Mystery would appear as absent from a world and life so amenable to constant remaking. And yet the bindingness of this vision of reality and of life, in terms of which this constant overcoming through the revelation of what is as amenable to it can take place, is indeed a mystery, one with the mystery of the givenness of all worlds and forms of humanity.

The revelation of this ultimate mystery, of the transhistorical mystery of the givenness of human life as uncovering what is, of mystery as the ultimate source of the authority of our forms of life and of the reality they reveal for us, is possible with the appearance of the historicality of worlds and their forms of humanity. This manifests itself through this mutation, in its difference from modernity and what preceded it. Paradoxically, the ultimate concealment of mystery reveals it. The 'final accounts of reality' of the visions in terms of 'permanent presence' are revealed, in their claim on us, as historically contingent, which then opens the possibility of attempting to think the nature of this history and so of the origin of this claim.

The 'history of Being', the tradition of raising the 'whole' within which and of which we live to an explicit vision, is formed in terms of the increasing concealment of the essential role of concealment, mystery, in our sense of the reality of ourselves and our world. Only this provides the authority for our uncovering of what is as binding. This is experienced at the inception of this tradition, but the conditions for such experience, in the giving of humanity as the clearing, is not addressed. The tradition unfolds as the attempt to make the 'whole' present, graspable, fully understandable by us. In this process, there is a constant reinterpretation of the 'authority' which the notion of reality embodies. From the address of what is to the early Greeks, to the givenness of the unchangeable Forms, to the Forms in the mind of the creator God, and so to Reason which the world embodies and in which we participate, the 'whole' is increasingly understood as 'illuminated', lacking concealment. This finds its ultimate form in the contemporary mutation of the tradition, where the 'whole' is no longer a matter of complete illumination for representation but rather is formed in terms of a constant will to overcome the appearance of givenness, the resistance to mastery. Yet all these forms reveal 'reality' in different ways only because they are human projects of forming what is ultimately given in the giving of humanity as the clearing of what is. Only because we and reality are already constantly given in unreflective factical life can there be projects of taking over this primordial givenness in different ways. Only so can reality appear as oriented towards the Forms or towards the Creator God, as formed in terms of universal law, or indeed as resource for endless remaking. With this last permutation, the historicality of the tradition becomes manifest and opens up the possibility of recovering a relation to this primordial givenness in a way which goes beyond the early Greek experience of concealment.

This is the revelation of what Heidegger calls 'Appropriation', *Ereignis*, the belonging together of the human and Being, that the human being is essentially the 'clearing' within which beings, both itself and others, can presence, and that this is given. We must enter into this primordial belonging, come to experience the primordial way in which reality manifests itself in human living and bring

this to language. This requires a 'turning away from the attitude
of representational thinking' ('The Principle of Identity' in *Identity
and Difference*, trans, J. Stambaugh, New York,1969, (hereafter *ID*,)
p. 32). The first beginning *opened up* the familiar world *as* world,
as a whole, in the revelation of its otherness, its claim on us. This
opened up world, world as world, becomes then the object of a
project to make it 'present', to grasp the nature of reality as such.
This trajectory is characterized, therefore, by 'representational
thinking', the attempt to stand over against the 'whole' in thought
as ultimately intelligible. To give up representational thinking is
to enter rather into a *receptive* relation, releasement (*Gelassenheit*), to
the mystery of the givenness of human life as revelatory of what
is. 'We must experience simply this owning in which man and
Being are delivered over to each other, that is, we must enter into
what we call *the event of appropriation (Ereignis)'* (*ID* p.36). We need to
recover the sense of a transformative experience and its revelation
of the givenness of the familiar world, but now in a reflection from
within this transformation on the context within which it can take
place. Here the experience is no longer of 'beings as beings' (as
other, unconcealed out of concealment), but as 'things'. A 'thing'
(which can be anything which presences within our world) gathers
the context whose givenness constitutes the belonging together of
the human and being. In the transformative experience we leave
behind, as Heidegger puts it, all claim to the unconditioned (that
is, to the ground of the whole which we can grasp) and recognize
our fundamental 'conditionedness', the givenness of ourselves and
our world out of the mystery ('The Thing' in *Bremen and Freiburg
Lectures*, trans. A. Mitchell, Bloomington, 2012, p.19 (hereafter
BF)). To live in this way is to 'dwell'. To dwell is to live as mortals
(the givenness of human life in its nature as revealing what is),
on the 'earth' (within a non-human environment which is only
ever partially revealed by our activities and so contains essential
concealment which we must recognize and preserve in our
relation to it), under the 'sky' (the primordial giving of 'time' to
us as mortals living on the earth in the alternation of day and
night, the passing of the seasons, and so forth, and which we must

reflect in our everyday lives (we 'do not turn night into day, not day into harassed unrest')), and before the 'gods' (the givenness of the meaningfulness for us of our most important forms of life, that we 'receive' this meaning, it is not a consequence of our choice or desire: we do not 'make ((our)) gods for ((ourselves)) and do not worship idols' ('Building, Dwelling, Thinking' in *BW*, p. 328).

This would be a 'new beginning', a relation to what made the 'history of Being' possible (the oblivion of this context for the appearance of the otherness of the familiar world to the Greeks) and so in that sense a relation to the ahistorical (the giving of the human and the world the concealment of which leads to the 'epochs' of that history), a 'liberation from history' (*Country Path Conversations*, trans. B.W. Davis, Bloomington, 2016, p. 120).

BT had endeavoured to return us to the 'primordial' way in which beings and ourselves are present to us, prior to any reflective appropriation of them philosophically or scientifically (in the broad German sense which encompasses natural, social and humanistic inquiry). This 'primordial' way is in 'factical life', our everyday purposive existence in which we take over forms of life in response to the issue which our lives are for us. In living this life we 'uncover' beings and ourselves. We can thematically uncover them in statements or experiences only because we first do so in our factical life in which we inhabit 'worlds' structured in terms of 'worldhood'. Inhabiting such environments we uncover 'equipment' in their references to each other, and these chains of references have their direction in relation to the human purposes which are lived out there. And this in turn points us to the wider human and non-human environment which forms their background context. The understanding of world and worldhood in constituted here by human purposive living. It is 'opened up' in breaks in that living, revealing the network of references involved, which can then be reflectively appropriated. We take over the tradition of explicitly understanding the 'whole' by understanding it *from* factical life, from our everyday existence: we understand ourselves as Being-in-the-world, as existing beings having their lives to live through taking over forms of life lived in environing worlds.

But now, this vision of BT undergoes a 'turn', to take over the 'whole' in terms of the *giving* of human life as the 'clearing' within which what is can appear. This is still to understand the 'whole' from out of our everyday existence, the way things are given to us in our ordinary unreflective purposive existence. But now this 'whole' is formed in terms of the giving of Dasein as 'clearing' and the reality it uncovers in living that life, out of mystery. 'We name the appropriating mirror-play of the single field of the earth and sky, divinities and mortals, the world' ('The Thing' *BF*, p. 18), World here is the whole in which the human form of life as given ('mortals'), is lived in terms of a significance which it does not create ('divinities'), in an encompassing non-human environment which life only ever partially uncovers ('earth') within the context of a primordially given temporality ('sky'). We relate to what presences within this world as a 'thing' when we experience it as pointing us to these dimensions and so to the mystery which underlies life and the reality it uncovers. We 'dwell' when a relation to this mystery informs our living and so transforms our everyday factical existence: no longer 'authenticity' as self-transformation, but 'releasement' to the mystery.

3.

In *Being and Time*, being and time are understood in terms of the individual Dasein taking over their lives in the face of death. Dasein is living temporality, and realizes its individuality in living towards death, in authentically taking over its finitude. This opens up the past as the repository of possibilities for Dasein's resolute choice of a way to be, of choosing its 'hero', and opens the future as unconstrained by previous choices and inauthenticity. Dasein's living temporality is understood either as that of 'das Man', in which Dasein's concrete way to be is already determined by social convention so the past is finished, the future closed and the present that of acting out the determined social role, or of authenticity. Beings, 'what is', are what is uncovered in living Dasein's temporality. That temporality is what gives the 'present' within which what is can presence, be manifest. The Being of beings is the form such beings take in terms of Dasein's living its ways to be: ready to handedness, present at handedness, and the existentiality of Daseins.

But when the inquiry turns to focus on the giving of Dasein as the clearing within which beings can presence and so be a measure of thought and action, having authority for Dasein, then temporality must be rethought. This 'giving' is presupposed in any uncovering of what is, of what presences. But it is not to be understood as something given and completed, in the sense this might have within a Medieval perspective, as creation. Rather, it is the constant giving which characterizes human life as the uncovering of what is. This is the 'ahistorical' time of the mystery, relation to which is 'releasement'. But this points to the problem of expression here. We are trying to talk of what makes any talking, any comportment to what is, possible, and so any form of expression is directed, not to describing, but rather to opening us to an experience of the mystery of human life and its world. The human 'belongs to Appropriation ...This is why we can never place Appropriation in front of us, neither as something opposite us nor as something all encompassing'; 'The awakening to Appropriation must be experienced, it cannot be proven ... experiencing is nothing mystical, not an act of illumination, but rather the entry into dwelling' (*On Time and Being'*, trans. J. Stambaugh, London, 1972, pp. 23, 53). Such experience gives us nothing to grasp, but rather opens us to dwelling, to living in terms of a fundamental relation to mystery in our lives. It is this relation which gives the measure for the temporal as it gives measure for the temporality of human life itself. In the inception of the 'history of Being' this ahistorical time is glimpsed in the claim which the otherness of the familiar world makes in the experience of wonder. The claim 'addresses' us, and so comes from a 'source' beyond the presencing beings. But that glimpse itself is concealed where relating to 'the whole' becomes a project of making present, of making it available to our grasp. There the measure for the temporal becomes initially an intelligible structure which as measure is eternal and unchanging, and, as understandable, is permanent presence, the intelligible structure of the *kosmos*. This intelligibility, for the world of later antiquity, does not go all the way down, forming as it does unintelligible matter. Permanent presence transmutes in Medieval understanding to the mind of the eternal creator God, where the totality of the temporal is open to view and to judgement. Within modernity, this vision of a completely intelligible universe for a self-creating God becomes transposed to the autonomous and self-illuminated subject standing over against an (in principle) intelligible world, intelligible because it is to be understood through the human's own projection of law. The subject and the world are in this way (in principle) permanently present. The permanent presence of the structure of the *kosmos,* of God's creation, and of the law governed universe, gives worlds of 'absolute truth' where the human relates to reality as having a final account. This sense of subjection to an ultimate measure or standard for human life and thought and its associated sense of a 'final account' is, for Heidegger, undermined by the transition of the modern world to that of the 'Age of Technology', in which the projection of permanent presence is transmuted to the projection of what is as resource for endless remaking. Here reality is uncovered as endlessly reformulable in terms of human will and its projection of overcoming its past, so that the very idea of something fixed becomes itself a provocation. The permanent presence of the measure for the temporal here becomes the provocation to overcoming which is always presupposed in any revealing of what is as resource. As beyond intelligibility, it is one might say a reverse image of the mystery to which releasement invites us. What is concealed by this provocation, however, is the very giving of this trajectory, of will to will as a way to be for Dasein and resource as a way reality may manifest itself. This giving cannot be overcome. It is as the transhistorical mystery of the giving of Dasein's way to be and the reality it reveals.

This tradition is the 'oblivion of Being' in the sense that it fails to understand the 'whole' in terms of the primordial way 'reality' is given to us in our everyday purposive lives, focusing rather on the 'beings' revealed in life. The task for us now is to recover this insight, to think the whole from out of the recognition of the 'oblivion of Being'.

This certainly makes it sound as if we can only relate to the 'whole' in terms of mystery by going through such a reinterpretation of the tradition of Western thought. And, as we've seen, there are passages which seem to point in that direction (for example, *The End of Philosophy*, pp 59, 61, quoted above). But that would seem to make our current response dependent on an interpretation which must be open to question, and therefore only to be held conditionally. Yet what Heidegger tries to get us recognize, and open ourselves to, is releasement to the mystery of our condition as world dwellers, which is at least a releasement from all demands for reasons. We recognize that all giving of reasons depends ultimately on the giving of our nature as revealing what is, which is itself without reason, the mystery. The way towards this is, we might say, a shedding of the demand for reasons, a releasement from the demands of the tradition, demands which would only be continued if we insisted that we must justify this in terms of a reinterpretation of that tradition. Indeed, in coming into relation to the mystery, 'a liberation from history could come about' (*CPC* p.120). We come into relation to the ahistorical. (It is this which makes possible Heidegger's later interest in Eastern Asian thought, and provides the basis for surmising that such a relation to mystery is a constant possibility for humanity.) This means that, as with the earlier writings, we can be opened to the experience of what Heidegger calls Appropriation from within our current life. One way would no doubt be through being struck by the historicality of previous philosophical claims to articulate the structure of reality, suggesting the hubris and confusion of such an ambition. But there seems no reason why we should not be able to experience a fundamental disposition comparable to the Early Greek experience of wonder which opens up our life to a recognition of its mystery and which could provide the basis for reflection on, and articulation of how, that life and its world now appears. One might question, then, why Heidegger confines his treatment of wonder to its role in the inception of Greek thought.

Indeed, he appears to deny that we can experience wonder, at least in a comparable way to the Greeks. For us 'the basic disposition, which would primordially displace man again into beings as a whole, is absent and denied us'; 'the basic disposition can no longer be the one of wonder, in which beings as such with regard to their Being once emerged as the most unusual' (*BQ* pp158, 159). But perhaps this suggests that wonder now must take a different form to that experienced by the Greeks, given that we have lived within a culture informed by the history of philosophy. Whatever Heidegger's thought here, it is difficult to see why wonder may not function for us as a fundamental disposition which can open up the vista within which a relation to the givenness of Dasein as the clearing for what is out of mystery can be formed. Indeed, there may be other ways in which we can experience Appropriation, as we shall see in the next chapter. For it still remains the case that in the later writings philosophical reflection proceeds as a development of our concern with our own being, that it is mine and so I have a concern with the kind of being I am, and that the possibility of this development is occasioned by breaks in our ordinary immersive life. Wonder at the world and life may constitute such a break, opening up the view on beings as such and as a whole. It may thus open up, we might think, the vista within which the very givenness of Dasein as the clearing for what is and so of our world can become manifest. There would be unconcealed the mystery of this giving itself, as the mystery, opening us to the possibility of entering into 'releasement'. But this possibility, one might think, in being intrinsic to our ordinary life, may be actualized in many ways. 'The one thing thinking would like to attain …is something simple. As such Being remains mysterious, the simple nearness of an unobtrusive governance' ('Letter on Humanism', *BW* p. 212). In the next chapter I will be looking at examples of ways in which we may become aware, and enter explicitly into, this 'governance'.

4.

This exposition of what I take to be the central tendencies of Heidegger's thought raises issues which need further elaboration if the claim for the centrality of mystery in understanding the human condition is to be persuasive. I would enumerate the following:

1. Understanding the sense of 'the whole' in which we live and of which we are a part is obviously central to Heidegger's thought both early and late. What is the necessity of such an understanding, for the most part implicit in our lives?

2. Given that it is in terms of such understanding that we can justify our lives and our understanding of the beings we uncover in living them, are such understandings of 'the whole' themselves accountable? And if not, how is their persuasive force to be understood?

3. What is the nature of the primordial way in which beings and ourselves are manifest within which we may have an experience of 'Appropriation'?

4. This in turn relates to the availability of the experience of Appropriation. If it is not to be accessible purely to intellectuals able to recover the origins of the Western philosophical tradition, how is it manifest in life? Are there practices which are particularly conducive to such an experience? Can we see its recognition in other times, and in other traditions, given that Heidegger characterizes it as 'ahistorical'?

5. In terms of this understanding of 'the whole', what form of life would be lived through its recognition?

I want now to take up these questions in the context of the work of David E Cooper where we find elaborated a 'vision of mystery'.

Chapter 3

David Cooper: towards a recovery
of the sense of mystery.

In the introduction to *The Measure of Things* (Oxford, 2002), David Cooper says that he isn't setting out to 'demonstrate' the truth of 'the doctrine of mystery' with which the book culminates, nor the 'wrongheadedness' of positions incompatible with it, those he terms 'raw humanism' and 'absolutism' in their various forms. Rather, the most he hopes to achieve is to render his criticisms and his positive proposals 'plausible', although the latter he suspects 'will ...only be found compelling by people already 'attuned' to experiencing the world in a particular way. But that, I also suspect, ...is the lot of any philosophical proposals that, in effect, are urging something like a vision' (p. 20). Such 'visions' are understandings of how human beings are related to the world in which they live and which they conceptualize and describe. Understanding their nature and necessity will reveal the ground for Cooper's reservations concerning the reception of his 'vision of mystery'.

In an interview for 3ammagazine (at 3ammagazine.com *The Measure of Things*), Cooper suggests that the 'abiding and central concern of philosophy and religion alike' is 'the fear that the world is alien to human beings '. Such a fear arises with human self-reflection. We may guess, he writes (*World Philosophies*, Oxford, 2003, p. 5), that when such self-reflection arose, humans became conscious of their 'strangeness, of respects in which, for all their affinity with the animal and wider material world, they were set apart in it'. Indeed, this very capacity for self-reflection manifests this difference, for through it, our lives and our relation to the world become an issue. We realize that, fundamental to human life, unlike other forms, is the requirement of *accountability*. 'We are creatures for whom the kind of life to be lived matters as an issue' (*Existentialism*, Oxford, 2000, p. 74). We try to resolve this issue through adopting forms of living in the world. Humans are 'inveterately teleological creatures' (*MT*, p. 261), engaged, and consciously so, in life projects, such as raising a family, pursuing a career, and so forth, which involve an orientation to the distant future and a concern with one's past, which again marks our distinction from other forms of life (*WP*, p. 5). Such long term projects give point and structure to other activities in life. Projects such as these involve evaluation: they can be done more or less well, and so invoke some conception of a measure in terms of which this evaluation can be made. But further, no one could see such projects as giving point and worth to their life 'without regarding what he is trying to achieve, and how, as subject to measure' (*MT*, p. 263), as worthwhile. Such projects do not achieve their worth for us because we engage in them; we engage with them because we regard them as worthwhile. Further, such projects are lived in the world and so presuppose beliefs and general understandings of the world which must be warranted if the projects are to have the significance claimed for them. We are accountable in this way for our lives and so for our relation to the world. Self-conscious teleological existence requires a measure for human projects in terms of which their worthwhileness can be seen, and for beliefs and understandings of the reality in which they are carried out. 'We need conceptions to answer to something 'beyond the human' because we need the comportments that presuppose them to be answerable' (*MT* p. 352). The unity of the human with the world is to be found in some 'measure' for this accountability.

For us to do anything, there must be a 'space of possibilities', possible forms of life, and for this there must already be a sense of what is worth doing, and available 'moods' and 'attunements' that mean certain aspects of our world assume an attractive, repellent or related appearance. There must already be 'a light in which they show up for us in the way they do and invite us to treat them in this or that way' (*A Philosophy of Gardens*, Oxford, 2006, pp 145-7). Such an understanding of worthwhile ways to be and of the world must already form the context in which the individual may take on projects and act. This context is not of our doing, 'but is rather the condition of our doing anything'. (Cooper adds here, and this will assume central importance later, that 'what is responsible for all this being in place' cannot 'be described or conceptualized ...since it is the condition for the possibility of any descriptive terms or concepts with which we manage to equip ourselves' (*PG*, p. 147)). What is needed as measure for our projects and beliefs about the world is some 'general understanding of the world and ourselves', of our place in the world and so of the appropriate comportment of the human being to their lives and to the world in which they live. That is, some form of understanding which removes the 'fear' of alienation, which shows the world as an appropriate place for beings like us to live worthwhile lives. Such an overall understanding, for example the Augustinian, which underlay Medieval life, that the world and ourselves are created by God who has given us the resources to see at least part of the order of the world and the ability to identify His purpose for us, gives a sense of what is worthwhile doing (projects which direct us towards the Creator and prepare us for eternity) and not worthwhile (inquiry into nature beyond what is given to our intelligence as the ordering of the world evident to normal sensory experience), and the associated moods conformable with such an apprehension of life and the world (acceptance of what God gives, humility before God's infinite power and knowledge, and so forth). We shall return shortly to this vision. Within the context of such a given understanding of the place of humanity in the world, projects and purposes can be justified as can the beliefs and comportments to the world in which they are to be carried out.

Such general understandings of our place in the world, which may be developed and articulated in philosophy and religion, are obviously not merely 'intellectual' issues. Rather, humans need to understand their place in the world in order to live their lives as an 'issue' and so as accountable. For the most part, no doubt, such an understanding is taken for granted, implicit in the forms of life into which one is initiated in one's culture. But the ways in which the issue of our place in the world is resolved 'reflect and shape emotions, attitudes and comportment towards the world' (interview). Such understandings are what Cooper calls 'vital' matters. And one can perhaps now see the reason for his disclaimers in the introduction to *The Measure of Things*. Such understandings of our place in the world as the basis for accountability, for giving justification for our projects and beliefs and conceptions of the world, are not themselves accountable to something further, at least in terms of the lived nature of those understandings. For someone living in the context of the Augustinian vision, it is not itself 'accountable' but rather that in terms of which any accountability takes place. Cooper's 'doctrine of mystery' is an alternative 'vision'. Coming to see life and the world in its terms is to change one's comportment to them and so come to have different 'vital' relations, dispositions and emotions. Coming to see life and the world in terms of such a vision is to undergo something more akin to the 'turning around of the soul' said to characterize religious conversion. It is not a matter of accepting arguments in terms of one's existing standards of accountability, but of entering into a new sense of what accountability can mean. Philosophy emerges as an explicit questioning directed towards the measure which can unify human life with the world of its understanding. In *The Measure of Things*, Cooper outlines the careers of three forms of such 'vision', of understandings of our place in the world, in Western life and thought, while expounding his 'doctrine of mystery' by reference in particular to Eastern traditions of Daoism and Buddhism. 'Absolutism' sees life and understandings of the world as subject to the measure of a discursable reality 'as it any way is', conceptually independent of human life, while for 'humanism' no such notion of reality is intelligible, all conceptions of the real being formed in accordance with human interests and purposes. For the vision with which Cooper identifies, 'ineffabilism', any describable world is indeed only intelligible in relation to human life, but that world is subject to the measure of an ineffable reality beyond the human.

Cooper's account of the unfolding of this history, and why it culminates for him in the 'doctrine of mystery', can be illuminated by his discussion of Heidegger's 'History of Being'(in *Heidegger*, London, 1996). This history has 'epochs' which broadly correspond with the delineation of historical forms of absolutism and humanism in *The Measure of Things*. But, as Cooper emphasizes, and as we have already seen, Heidegger in using the term 'epoch' is playing on the Greek term *epoche* meaning 'withdrawal'. These 'epochs' are ways in which 'Being' increasingly withdraws. We can get a sense of what this might mean in recalling the beginnings of the tradition of Western philosophy. If we think of Plato's work as a 'search for home' in the world which inspired the wonder he expresses, then for Heidegger this search has with Plato already gone astray. The 'world' with which we are to be in unity appears to Plato as one of distinct beings, so that the direction of the project to avert alienation lies in trying to show that such beings are *thinkable*, and so, to some degree thought like, and in that way one with us. The world is not alien because it can be intellectually encompassed by us in the sense that the world of experience is subject to the measure of the purely intelligible, the Forms. But for Heidegger this forgets how it is possible for there to be distinct beings to think: how it is that such beings become manifest at all. As we have already noted, for Heidegger, such beings become manifest only where the stream of life in the world is broken. That stream is a 'process, of arising, of emerging from the hidden' (Heidegger *Introduction to Metaphysics*, pp14-15, quoted *H.* p. 63) of things, articulated, as we have seen, in the pre-Socratic notion of *physis*, a 'self-blossoming emergence' of things. Beings are experienced as such as self emergent, as 'unconcealed' in relation to concealment, and so from within the context of human activity. Human life is given measure by being entrusted with preserving unconcealment, in resisting what may distort the self-manifestation of beings. It is this self emergence from concealment, within human activity, that is the nature of 'truth' (*aletheia*) not, as with Plato, conformity to some measure beyond the living of human life. Nevertheless, the focus of the early Greek thinkers was still on 'beings', on how their 'reality' as beings was to be understood and related to, and not on the nature of what made such unconcealment possible. In that sense, Western thought begins in the 'oblivion of Being'. The 'History of Being' shows the way this 'oblivion' provokes ever increasing attempts at 'being at home' through the *domination* of the beings which are the focus of attention, rather than how it is that there are beings at all. The positions, the various 'visions', involve our work, of course, but that is a response to a situation which is not of our doing. The initial reflective appropriation through the experience of wonder in early Greek thought opened beings as revealed in *physis*, as claiming us in living practices, as both experienced and beyond experience, but did not reflect on the the fundamental form of unconcealment, the *giving* of human life as revelatory of beings, how it is possible for there to be beings for us at all. This remained concealed, precipitating us on a course of trying to recover our 'oneness' with the universe in ways which necessarily fail. In each failure, reality shows itself to us as alien in a new way, creating a context which invites renewed attempts at dominion and so leading us further astray, until the process culminates in the 'homelessness' of 'the Age of Technology' where all beings including ourselves appear as resources for the unsatisfiable 'will to will'. We will return to this characterization of our current predicament. Western humanity's drive to be at home in the world, and so 'accountable', results in homelessness in a radical sense, with the complete oblivion of Being as emergence, with the loss of any sense of mystery, in the appearance of 'what is' as a 'standing reserve' for formation in terms of whatever we will.

The first part of *The Measure of Things* outlines the careers of the visions of absolutism and humanism from the Medieval Augustinian understanding to the present. It is important to understand this development, not merely in terms of resolutions to an intellectual problem ('what is the nature of reality?', say) but as responses to a disquiet as to the meaningfulness of life. The question as to the measure in terms of which life is meaningful is one which concerns our fundamental attunements to the world and our relation to our own lives. The issue is, then, a 'vital' one, and these 'vital issues are not to be identified without attention to the moral and other significance with which the thesis and it precursors have actually been invested' (*M 1, p. 22*).

The Augustinian vision is a paradigmatic absolutist resolution to the issue of the human's relation to reality which provides a measure for human life and human understanding of the world. The world and human being are the creation of God whose purposes for us and design of the world are at least partially available to us through the use of our reason. The world is created to serve humanity and point human life to the Creator. The world has an order both natural and moral which is for the good of humanity (*MT*, p. 30). This understanding was not merely a matter of intellectual concern but informed the life of Medieval Christians, determining the conceptually available notions of what was worthwhile and what the standard for the truth of beliefs and understanding of the world was. Human life was given worth by its nature as created, a life to be lived in accordance with the evident purposes of God revealed by reason and Scripture. Beings in the world were created in accordance with the Ideas in the mind of God which provide, to the extent we have rational access to them, the standard for belief and understanding. This vision of 'home' (in the eternal) alienated humanity from temporal life. The essential part of humanity is that which allows it to relate to the transcendent God, so that the body and the 'animal functions' appear as the 'enemy' to be controlled by ascetic practices. Human aspiration should be directed towards the contemplation of the divine ideas to the extent this is possible in this life and in the hope and expectation of fulfillment in the hereafter. In relation to the natural world, the tendency, as noted above, was to believe that the world, without too much human intervention, would function for our good as it had been designed for us. From the human point of view, no doubt this involved the infliction of many unwanted things, disease, drought, accidents, and so on, the connection of which to the human good was opaque, but this was, given the limited extent of our understanding of God, to be expected. Natural science, in the sense of systematic, purposive enquiry into the regularities governing the world was either redundant (the standard of truth lay with the divine ideas) or offensive, since classificatory schemes produced to further our desires could only lead us away from the truth (*MT*, p. 37).

The hold of this vision of the human place in the universe is loosened and with it the confidence in the intelligibility of the world and of our place in it through a 'fascination' with God's infinite power and freedom (H. Blumenberg quoted *MT* p. 26), one which finds articulation in Ockham and associated thinkers. Again, the human work in articulating and developing how reality and life appears now is dependent on that appearance which is not of our doing. Rather it is, as noted above, a consequence of the hidden trajectory of the tradition of understanding human life and the world, in suppressing a sense of mystery in the drive towards making the 'vision' present to human understanding. This drive reveals the failure of the Augustinian vision to unify the human with the universe at large in terms of a Creator God. God's freedom and power make Him inscrutable to human capacities since His purpose in giving us these capacities remains unknowable. Reality and life begin to show themselves in a new light. The world no longer mirrors Divine Ideas, accessible in part to human reason, but is a realm of absolute contingency subject to a Divine will whose contours lie beyond our understanding. The world may, for all we know, be structured quite otherwise than we believe. We can no longer be confident that the world was created for our good in any sense of the word we can understand: 'good' is determined by the Divine Will of which we can have no comprehension. This vision undermines the assumption of our living in a divinely ordered universe which is at least partially understandable by us and in which we can live according to divinely ordered purposes to aspire to union with God, a vision which formed the understanding of the worth of human life and the standard for beliefs about the world for the Medieval Christian. The new vision precipitated a profound sense of alienation, of living in a divinely created world without the assurance that, as finite intelligences, we had any true understanding of our role in it.

This situation in turn provoked a 'self-assertive' response, finding 'knowledge' and life's goals within the powers of human determination. This move, which underlay the new forms of life emergent in the Renaissance, was not in itself an irreligious one: rather it was seen as an emulation of God's creativity within the context of human life. A new valuing of creativity and purposeful activity and of the body as essentially involved in productive activities emerged. With this new sense of the human significance of creative and productive activities went a valuing of active intervention in nature and inquiry into the regularities of the natural world. A new concern with securing and improving human material well-being ensued, and since we can no longer refer to a divinely ordained natural law, guidance for human life was sought from human resources, custom, history, and common sense.

But such a purely human response to the issue of alienation is unsatisfactory. Without knowledge of divine sanction for the forms of human worth and understanding, they were always open to skeptical disquiet. The very success of the emerging sciences, technical improvements and artistic triumphs of the Renaissance, however, suggested a way out, in prompting the thought that such success must be due to our divining the order of the created universe, discovering the laws of nature and beauty. A renewed belief that rational inquiry can uncover God's order, the discursable order of reality 'as it anyway is', developed, with an added confidence that such understanding need not be, as it was for the Medieval mind, essentially partial and constricted by our finite condition. The proliferation of rational systems claiming to reveal 'reality as it is' suggested, however, that such confidence was misplaced. This dawning sense found explicit articulation in Kant's restriction of the claims of metaphysics to articulating the conditions under which experience of objects is possible while recognizing that knowledge of 'things in themselves', independent of the human perspective or of the perspective of any being relating to the world in terms of sensory experience, was impossible.

This was, however, as a response to the possibility of alienation, unstable and invited skeptical questioning. Objects in the world must be understood in terms of the forms of space and time and in terms of certain categories, in particular substance and causality, but these do not apply to 'things in themselves'. We are certainly, in one way, in the world, and as such must be understood in terms of causal laws. This seems to put our freedom and so morality in question. But we cannot be just objects in the world, since we are the 'for whom' there is a world of objects at all. Freedom and morality are possible if we think of ourselves in a two fold way, as belonging to the world of sense but also as noumena, intelligences, 'things in themselves' subject only to the laws of reason. But this bifurcation of the self and of reality into the realm of objects and 'things in themselves' seems the articulation of a new form of alienation. We may by reason know the categorical imperative and that we are free, but we must act in the world: how is free action possible in a world governed by causal laws? (A problem we have seen resurface in Wittgenstein's *T*: how can the vision of the 'happy man' be enacted in the world of facts?) And why shouldn't the bifurcation of reality lead to skeptical thoughts: even if our world must appear to us in this way, why isn't it merely a veil of illusion before a reality that is necessarily inaccessible to us?

Such a new sense of alienation precipitates a 'Promethean' response articulated in different ways by Marx and Nietzsche. It is human activity in response to need and purposes which is the constructive source of the 'human world' (*MT*, p. 81) and no sense can be attributed to a 'reality as it is in itself'. There is only the world constituted by human practices, and so it is not a world merely of appearances or 'phenomena' contrasted with the way things are in themselves. It is 'reality'. What distinguishes the human being is the creative agency embodied in human projects and activities in terms of which the world appears and is understood. The human being should therefore live as a creative agent, as a 'free spirit' (Nietzsche) or as 'species life' (Marx) in which they regard the world as their product. We should recognize the natural world in this way and act accordingly. However, there is an ambiguity in these forms of 'Prometheanism' as to the position of the human agent. Both Marx and Nietzsche want to see the human being as 'natural', as one 'among the animals' as Nietzsche put it (*MT*, p. 80). But how can human beings be responsible for there being a discursable world and at the same time be merely items in that world?

The movement of thought Cooper calls 'Existential Humanism' abandons the naturalism of Prometheanism and the talk of the world as something we 'create' or make (*MT*, p.101) while carrying forward the understanding that the concepts we apply to the world are formed in terms of human interests and valuations, and the things to which the concepts are applied are intelligible only in relation to our purposive practices. No 'sense can be made of what it is for something to exist except as 'concerning us' '(*MT*, p.100). We are, in the early Heidegger's formulation, 'Being-in-the-world', essentially and not just contingently always already relating to beings in our activities. No sense can be made, therefore, of our being essentially cut off from the world, necessitating an explanation of how contact with the world is possible. We can reflect on things and ourselves, but detachment presupposes the primacy of active practical engagement in the world with things. Such engagement manifests an understanding which has its own knowledge, knowing how to move and deal with things as they are manifest in the practical environments in which we live. Things are meaningful in so far as they concern us: they are encountered within the conduct of our practical activities. To speak of 'meaningfulness' here is to speak of the way any meaningful item refers to others. 'In unreflectively, though not blindly and without intelligent purpose, taking hold of the broom, I am directed towards the floor-dust for whose removal brooms are designed, and hence to the state the house should be in if other domestic activities, like cooking, are to be properly conducted. Through such activities, I am referred to my family with whom I eat, and hence to the ways of my society which shape when, where and how families eat together …Eventually, I am directed towards a whole 'Life' ' (*MT*, p. 115). In this way, in using the broom we are referred to the 'world' in Heidegger's sense of a 'relational totality', a 'structured whole of meaningful connections' (*MT*, p.116). Things which are not made to fulfill functions, 'natural' things, must also signify in this way: they are encountered primordially in their relation to our practical activities in the world so that, for example, winds 'are first 'discovered' in the context of activities like farming, where they serve to direct the farmer to the impending threat to his crops' (*MT*, p. 116). (This may seem exaggerated, but the point is that 'natural' phenomena are first revealed in human purposive activity. Clearly that activity revealed 'wind' prior to the development of farming!)

The Existential Humanist overcomes the alienation implicit in the Promethean stance through understanding the human being as Being-in-the-world, essentially immersed in the world through living forms of life into which she was inducted in becoming, in Heidegger's term, 'Dasein'. The world as such is uncovered in the mood of *Angst*, an experience of the sheer contingency of the world into which we are thrown. The world might have been different and there is no 'final vocabulary' in Richard Rorty's words to judge or question the validity of our conceptions. *Angst* is the experience of the groundlessness of our existence and of our world. In this way, it is the disclosure of our lack of *answerability* to any measure beyond that existence and world (*MT*, p.254) (reflected in the role of authenticity in *BT* as the way in which we embrace our finitude), and it is just this which marks this vision as another manifestation of homelessness. This humanism cannot be lived, Cooper claims, since we cannot regard the worth of our fundamental projects that structure our lives as deriving from our engagement in them, as proceeding, say, from 'authentic choice'. We commit ourselves, rather, because we regard these projects as worthwhile and so by reference to some measure beyond ourselves. Since that measure cannot lie in reference to some wider human circle of approval whose legitimacy can equally be questioned, appeal must be made to something 'non-human'. And similarly for the beliefs and understandings of the world involved in the pursuit of these projects and the life they structure. We cannot regard their 'truth' or justifiability as determined by reference to human agreement. But the issue of our answerability is not to be resolved by referring to 'the way the world any way is' for the Existential Humanist has rightly shown the unintelligibility of such a proposal. Rather, it is to be resolved by reference to 'mystery': to a reality beyond the human which is not therefore discursable. The 'truth of mystery …is this: any world we can articulate is a human world, shaped by our practices and purposes, not reality 'as such'. Yet we cannot but believe that there is a 'beyond the human' that is responsible for the arising of this world- something, that, since it does not belong in the human world, must be ineffable, mysterious' (*Senses of Mystery*, Abingdon, 2018, p. 24). It is to mystery, to the mysterious giving of our world, that we are accountable. The world is a 'referential totality' we inhabit in living the practices and purposes which give sense to the references in terms of which things have their identity. The mystery is the giving of the world we find ourselves in and so the giving of the beings revealed in living the possibilities made available by this world.

Any world that can be described is one formed in terms of human purposes and interests. 'Things stand out for us and light up for us- and for any other creatures- only through the significance they have within a web of life, a life that is charged with desires, goals and values. A world, one might say, is a theatre of significance' (*SM*, p.5). It is through such significance, how something matters to us, that it can be identified and fall under a concept (*MT*, p. 114). The world is, then, a world of *experience*: the forms of life structured in terms of human purposes and interests in which things can stand out, be 'lit up' for us, are *lived*, are the loci of experience. But for such structure to be *binding* on us, the world of experience must be 'given', have a source beyond it.

Our experience of the world is not primarily that of a detached observer but of purposive agents for whom things stand out in terms of our bodily engagement in the world. This engagement is of a peculiar intimacy with the things which 'light up' in this way. Cooper considers a vivid example of this intimacy in the reflection of sunlight on the sea: 'the light is not the object of a detached spectatorial gaze: rather the light reverberates with us, it transmits to us, penetrates us …At the same time, *what* we see is not an ingredient of reality that exists independently of our vision' (*Sunlight on the Sea*, no place of publication given, 2013, p.50). We are 'inscribed' by the reflections: we are receptive, they 'presence'. Yet their being as reflections depends on our capacities bodily and linguistic. To recognize this is to recognize our 'convergence with the world' (*SS*, p.51). Our intimacy with the world we experience in our unreflective but intelligent dealings in it finds expression in Merleau-Ponty's remark that to 'see the world is also …to feel oneself seen' (quoted *SS*, p.72). The experience of reflections on the sea is of seeing (reflections do not exist independently of our vision) and being seen (we are 'inscribed' by them), so that, in Merleau-Ponty's words, ' it is impossible to say that nature ends there and that man …starts here' (quoted *SS*, p. 71). In the primary way we are in the world, there is no separation of a 'subject' standing over against an 'object', of an 'interior sensation' and an 'external stimulus'. Of course, given this primary form of experience in the world, it is possible to detach oneself from it and take up a 'theoretical' stance of inquiring, say, into the physiological changes occurring in the experience. But that stance presupposes the way things are given primarily in experience.

Every experience in our engaged life in the world has this dual aspect. We are 'inscribed' and so receive what is in the world, while *what* that is is not independent of our practices. What we experience is 'given' to us, and yet depends on the nature of our practices and capacities. This 'givenness' is, therefore, at the same time of *us*. Our congruence with the world is 'not the givenness of the world to an 'us', a subjectivity already there, up and running: rather we too are 'given', our frameworks of belief and norms, our basic practices and our form of life no more our achievement than is the world which anyway cannot be prised apart from these ' (*MT*, p. 361). There is a constant giving of our congruence with the world, of us as, in Heidegger's term, the 'clearing', in the giving of the fundamental practices and forms of life which constitute our 'bodily' engagement in the world and constitute that world as a world of experience. The constant giving of congruence is thus recalled 'as emerging from a mysterious source, as an ineffable coming to presence for us of a world' (*SS*, p.88).

The 'source' is 'ineffable' as it is the giving of the describable world and so is prior to any possible description. But it is not separable from the world, which would make it susceptible to description: it is not a creator God. It is 'a mysterious arising of phenomena into the integrated realms of experience that we call worlds. Every experience presupposes this enigmatic process of arising: but equally, no sense can be made of the process- the source- except by reference to what arises or advances in and through it' (*SS*, p.80).

The world of experience is the world of living purposive practices and forms of life. It is then the world of possible forms of life and practices we can inhabit, 'the great open web of the world of experience' (*Convergence with Nature*, Totnes, 2012, p. 93). In experience, phenomena arise (we are inscribed). What presences is not an 'object' for a spectating view, but an item in the flow of congruence with the world. It has its identity in relation to others in the environment we inhabit, and that environment ultimately refers us to the 'world', the possible forms of life we can live. Cooper refers here to the Indian Buddhist thinker Nagarjuna's notion of *sunyata*, 'emptiness' :'No thing ...has 'own being', since it is what it is only in relation to everything else in the world- rather as a word has the meaning it does only through belonging to a complete language' (*SM*, p. 65). Things are what they are as presencing within the world of experience and so in their relations to, and differences, from others. At the same time, as *presencing*, they are experienced in terms of a giving of the world of experience. 'There is a disclosure that at once 'gives' a world and 'gives' us. This is, to be sure, a 'human world' in which nothing 'lights up' except in relation to our practices and perspectives. But there is nothing human in what 'gives' a unity of world, practices and perspectives' (*MT*, p. 325). Within this giving, things presence relationally, 'pointing' to others, and so on indefinitely across the web of the world. They presence not as objects but rather in the manner of 'signs'.

Referring to the Daoist sage Zhuangzi, Cooper writes: ' openness to the mysteries of emergence and source is, as it were, the default, original condition of human beings. It is a condition from which they have fallen. As men and women have become ever more subject to the constraints of complex economies, sophisticated technologies, systems of scientific knowledge, cultural and intellectual fashions, and the frenetic business of city life, their sense of mystery has atrophied' (*SM*, p.66). (I will be considering the justification for this claim in chapter 5).

These are the constraints of forms of life which give priority to the theoretical appropriation of what presences in the world of experience, taking what theoretical approaches reveal as defining 'reality', and the forms of social, political and economic life which utilize the result of theoretical approaches to pursue the endless projections of human desire and whim. Theoretical approaches, in the broad sense, separate us from the flow of converged life to observe in a detached manner what presences there for the purposes of classification, prediction and control. But it is 'only because experience presents us with a world of trees, birds and other inhabitants of nature that scientists have anything in front of them to work on, to dissect, analyse and hypothesize about' (*SM*, p. 7). And it is that primordial world of experience which embodies the primary sense of 'reality'. Things 'are present 'just as they are', not despite the place they have in relation to our lives, but *through* this' (*PG*, p. 150). Science does not provide a privileged access to 'reality'. The accounts it gives are just as informed by human purposes as any other. 'The scientist describes the world from certain angles of interest- in the prediction and control of events, in taking things apart and making them, in finding cause and effect explanations, and so on. The concepts science deploys are shaped by such interests just as surely as the concepts used by art critics are shaped by very different concerns' (*CN*, p. 88).

Any reality we can describe and articulate is one formed in terms of human practices and interests. It is, therefore, a world of experience: 'any world we can think about and describe is not independent of how it is experienced' (*Sunlight on the Sea*, p. 77). But we must believe that there is a 'beyond the human' which is responsible for the arising of this world. The world as the world of emergent experience, the world we *live*, which manifests itself in the flow of life, is the 'primordial world'. The alienation which precipitated the search for 'home' in terms of control and domestication of beings emerged through a reflection which marked a radical break in the flow of life revealing a world of distinct objects over against the human subject. The attempts at recovering our unity with the world became attempts at uniting us with a world of objects, a project which through repeated failure results in the 'homelessness' of Heidegger's 'Age of Technology' in which all beings, including ourselves, appear as available, as resource for, the use and formation in terms of unsatisfiable will. Recovery from this requires recovery of what self-reflection had disrupted. This is, then, a 'recollection' rather than the acquisition of a new 'doctrine', reminding us of how things appear in the flow of life. We need to be recalled to the world of experience which is living life. This world when recovered, recollected, manifests itself as emergent from mystery.

How are we to be recalled to ourselves as living the world of experience, to experience 'primordial reality', to recover our convergence with nature? There are experiences, like that of the sunlight on the sea, Cooper calls 'epiphanies'. They 'play important, even indispensable roles in promoting our understanding of things' (*SS, p. 64*). An epiphany is an experience of the world which at the same time embodies the nature of that experience and so opens the latter, from within experience, for reflective appropriation. The experience of sunlight on the sea referred to above can be such an epiphany, one of our 'intimacy with nature', of the impossibility of saying where 'nature ends' and 'man starts'. 'The total, integrated experience of the play of the sun on water is an epiphany of the world as a whole. How the primordial world is shows up in this experience' (*SS, p.78*). Epiphanies play somewhat the role of the 'breaks' in 'factical life' in Heidegger's work. There the issue was to reveal the nature of 'unreflective life' without making it an 'object' for an external observer, but rather recognizing that the philosopher is herself immersed in that life. The need, therefore, is to allow the occasion for reflection to arise naturally within that life, and then to bring to reflection what is revealed in the vista thereby opened up, the dimensions of the 'lived world' or the lived experience of 'life as a whole'. Similarly here, epiphanies are experiences within the flow of the experiential world, which nevertheless break through its unreflective movement to open it to reflective appropriation.

There are practices which are peculiarly conducive to such epiphanies, and which may then be conducted, in a 'mindful manner', to cultivate and develop one's sense of the mystery of ourselves and our world. 'Walking, gardening, attention to animals, listening to the sounds of nature and music, watching the play of light and shadow' are examples (*SM, p. 2*). Different practices may be especially conducive to opening up particular aspects of that mystery, although they all, as themselves part of the giving of life and world, can intimate the nature of the mystery as such.

Engagement with animals can open us to the mystery of the particularity of our world of experience, that it is as it is. Animals are, to varying degrees, both comprehensible and opaque to us, the opacity deriving, not only from their different sensory capacities, but more from the form of their life, the concerns, purposes and relationships in terms of which they have their 'environing worlds'. We are confronted with different ways the world can be manifest, within a vision (our own) in which we recognize that we have no relation to 'reality as such' which would give ours priority. We can recognize the singularity of our vision 'cognitively', but living with animals converts this into living experience. (See *SM*, ch. 4, and *Animals and Misanthropy*, Abingdon, 2018).

Gardening can open us to the mystery of there being a world of experience at all in being an epiphany of that world itself. We 'make' a garden: it is a human practice or practices, which at the same time is in obvious ways dependent on 'nature', what is not of human making. But what gardening can bring to our awareness is that it is through human practices that 'natural' phenomena are manifest *as* 'natural': they appear, stand out, are significant only within such practices. Rain, weather, soil and plants are not there for us primordially as 'objects' for a disinterested gaze. They can become that, of course, but only because they are already there for us in a different way, manifest in the flow of purposive life. At the same time, 'cultural' phenomena, our appreciation of the beauty of the garden, its atmosphere, its originality in developing the possibilities of a particular tradition of gardening, and so on, are inextricably bound up with the 'natural'. The natural changes of light and shadow, weather and season, reveal the garden in ever, and constantly changing, new ways, which inform our appreciation of it so that we can't say 'nature ends there and that man …starts here' (Merleau-Ponty (ibid.). Further, the garden is not there as an 'object' for our appreciation: we are 'in' it, and walking around it reveals ever new aspects, gives us new experiences. The garden in this way, brings out, 'epiphanizes', one might say, the way we are in our world: the world is a human one, revealed through our bodily purposive activity, but it is at the same time 'given' from a source which must be mysterious.

Finally, Cooper suggests that walking can open us to an explicit experience of this source and be developed as a 'mindful' practice for 'reverie'. This is not walking for practical purposes, nor is it an opportunity for self-scrutiny. Rather, it is a 'relaxed' and 'mindful' way of walking recommended by the Daoist sage Zhuangzi, in which the rambler is 'liberated from the opposition 'self and other'', and hence is 'carried along by things so that the heart-mind wanders freely' (quoted *SM*, p. 57). For the meditative walker, the environment in which she walks is not an object for a spectator. She belongs to the environment. As she moves, she is part of an ever changing way the environment shows itself as an integrated landscape, the elements of which are understood in relation to each other and in relation to the walker. We are as meditative walkers part of an unfolding whole, in which, for example, deer, trees, grass, ponds, sky and clouds presence, manifest themselves in their relationality and in such a way that we are part of that manifestation. Further, they presence in relation to the wider context within which they have their identity: the tree 'points' to the earth, to the sun and rain, to the animals that eat its fruit and to the walkers who may rest in its shade. (These are, as Cooper recognizes, intimations of Heidegger's 'four-fold' of earth, sky, mortals and divinities we met in the last chapter). Through this we are led to the 'world' in which we live, the possible ways in which things can 'light up' for us. The entire world, as the Japanese Zen master Dogen said, 'manifests itself in a tall bamboo' (quoted *SM*, p.65). In meditative walking, we experience ourselves at one with the environment in an emergent presencing. 'The gathering together of things into a coherent, integrated environment through which the walker moves is a coming to presence that cannot be dissected and explained' (*SM*, p. 64). Through this we are led to an apprehension of the source of this emergence, 'an intimation of a mysterious well-spring from which it emerges' (*SM*, p. 66). Meditative walking can return us to an experience of the givenness of ourselves and the world we inhabit. Mindful walking is an exemplification of 'reverie', a practice which can be engaged with in other more sedentary ways. 'In reverie, a person sees things as they are …(it) is alertness-undistorted by prejudice, passion and purpose- to the places occupied by beings in the great open web of the world of experience' (*CN*, p.93). It is at the same time seeing this network, the world, as mysteriously given (*SM*, p.65). Reverie recalls us to a primordial experience of life in the world.

The epiphanies of sunlight on water, gardens and so forth, open up the primordial way we are in the world for reflective appropriation. We and the world arise constantly in experience, in the flow of purposive life. There is here no separation of 'subject' and 'object'. There is an arising ('phusis') which is spontaneous, but which can then be disrupted so that 'self' and 'object' may then manifest themselves and be available for description, explanation, prediction, and so forth. But without this spontaneous arising there would be no possibility of their appearance, their presence to us. To recognize this spontaneous arising is to recognize its mystery: it is a constant giving, the source of which is *the* mystery, one having no possible resolution as all such resolutions must lie within the disclosed world. As the source of a world which can be described, it is beyond any possible description: it is 'ineffable'. Epiphanies, and the 'reverie' which is mindful involvement in this spontaneous arising, embody a 'double exposure', a recognition that primordially the world, including ourselves, arise in experience, and that this arising is essentially mysterious. 'The world is the visible face presented to us by an ineffable 'coming' or 'advancing' of the source, the well-spring, of worlds of experience' *(SS p. 81)*.

How, then, might mystery be a measure for life? No doubt there are different emphases in traditions where this has been actualized (for example, in certain forms of Buddhism and Daoism which I will discuss in chapter 4) and others are no doubt possible. But what these traditions hold before us are lives (for example, of the Buddha or the Daoist sage) which exemplify in their characteristic virtues or excellences of character and the activities and actions which flow from these, such a relation to mystery. As we shall see in the next chapter, these exemplars do not constitute a 'goal' towards which we are to direct our efforts, but rather are to be contemplated and so to open ourselves to a recovery of the mystery which we *already* are. In this recovery we come to practice these excellences and so begin to acquire them, certain motivations, activities and actions begin to seem natural to us, as others lose their appeal and fall away. Cooper gives one sketch of such a life, that of the Daoist sage, in *Convergence with Nature (*pp 76-80*)*. If a relation to the mysterious giving of human life and its world is to be fundamental to life, a central excellence will be humility, a recognition that, whatever one's attainments, these depend on what is in no sense one's own achievement: the givenness of one's capacities, cultural inheritance, current social and historical situation, and above all on the very giving of oneself and one's world. The sage, then, 'is ...without a sense of himself as anything special' *(p. 76)*. And, seeing himself as part of the primordial giving of the world of experience, 'he does not see himself as an autonomous being set over and against the creatures which matter only as a means to the satisfactions of his wants and ambitions' *(ibid.)*. At the same time, he recognizes that as 'given', the human world of experience has no priority over the perspectives of other creatures. Humility is in this way productive of compassion, the recognition that other creatures have their own integrity and so are not to be seen as merely means for human ends.

Humility and compassion flow from his recognition that he is part of the unfolding coming to presence of the world. But further, that perception informs his understanding of his life as an 'imitation' of this constant giving of ourselves and our world, of the Dao, the unfolding of a process without purpose. Within the Eastern traditions of Daoism and Zen 'virtuous life is not only consonant with the truth of mystery, but may *emulate* the mysterious way of things' *(SM, p. 92)*. The world arises spontaneously in human bodily purposive life: the arising has no direction, no end. To imitate this, for the Daoist sage, is to embody the virtue of *ziran*, spontaneity. The sage's activities are not directed towards acquisition, dominated by fixed goals, but lived for their own sake, and in open receptivity to what may presence in the unfolding of the world. This responsiveness recognizes other living beings, both human and non-human, as having their own perspectives on the world, and, having himself, as part of the unfolding of world, a concern for their reality, the sage desires to help them realize their lives. As the mystery is the constant giving of worlds, emulating this involves energy, an open active engagement with the world. And that, for one attuned to mystery, will involve a sense of 'convergence with nature', that we and the world 'presence' together. To cultivate this, Cooper says, is indeed a virtue: 'To cultivate it is to cultivate a sense of kinship ...It is a virtue with an affinity to friendship' *(SS, p 53)*. (I shall examine in greater detail the nature of the Daoist position in the next chapter).

Positively, mystery can, therefore, give a 'measure' to life, in putting before us an understanding of the virtues of a life lived in giving it priority. Negatively, this vision is opposed to those which either deny any place to mystery, or which encourage and justify forms of life oblivious to it. Absolutism and uncompensated humanism are articulated versions of visions which to a greater or lesser degree deny or subordinate a relation to mystery. But our current cultural situation for Cooper is a toxic and incoherent combination of both. There is the presumption that only natural science gives us understanding and knowledge of the world (scientism), which could only be justified by the claim that it shows us 'reality as such', coupled with the belief that the application of this in technology is the primary means of achieving human goals (technologism). As to the latter, what is worth pursuing is identified with goals human beings themselves determine, unconstrained by any measure beyond them (humanism), while these goals themselves are always to be superceded in the name of progress (perfectionism). The combination of scientism and humanism gives us a sense of having a world, understood by science, controlled by technology, which is ours to do with as we will. Imbued with a sense of the mystery of life and the world, we would resist the dominance of this vision and its consequences.

We need, then, to be recalled, by epiphanies and articulation of the vision of life and world opened up there, to the 'primordial world' in order to resist the current dispensation. How, then, do 'beings' manifest themselves primordially?

The 'primordial world' is the world of living life. We are Being-in-the-world: our lives are essentially lived in engaging in projects and activities which are modes of engagement with beings beyond ourselves. Our relation to these beings is not primordially spectatorial: they are not 'objects' set over against us. They are revealed in our practical engagement which has its own understanding, 'operative understanding', of how to go about things in this environment. In living practices or forms of life, beings appear in terms of them and the purposes and interests which inform them. We encounter there beings as 'pointing' towards other beings including ourselves and others, and so in an ever widening relationship to encompass the range of possible forms of life which is available historically to us, one which we could live and so reveal beings through that life. Meditative walking, reverie, recollects this relationality in 'roaming' its connectivity, in wandering among the relations of things in our world.

In living practices, we are part of the stream of life in which we are not separate from the presencing of beings. This is a presupposition for any reflective appropriation of what presences: 'Once the intellect has got to work and carved this primordial world into discrete objects and structured patterns, we can predict and explain the occurrence of this or that experience. But before this happens, the world is experienced as spontaneous. Phenomena arise, merge, come apart, disappear in a fluid whole that is yet to fall victim to the mechanical models that human beings will eventually construct in order to rein in the spontaneous movement of experience' (*SS*, p.78). The stream of life is not an encountering with 'objects', although that can occur when the stream is broken, in encountering obstacles to its flow. In that flow, things presence inconspicuously, a presencing which is a pointing beyond in the relationality that is world. This presencing is 'spontaneous', it is emergent, involving both us and what presences. 'The phenomena that belong in this world are spontaneous, ephemeral, soft-edged, intimate with one another, and inseparable from the perspectives of the beings that experience them' (*SS*, p.78). This spontaneity is the emergence from mystery, a mysterious uprising. Cooper quotes the Zen master Dogen: 'something ineffable coming like this …an advancing (of) all things' (*SS*, p. 79).

It is, then, to the articulation of the 'vision of mystery' in Dogen and some central Daoist texts that I now turn.

Chapter 4

East Asian Origins

The first articulation of what I have called, following David Cooper, 'the vision of mystery' is found in certain Daoist writings of the Warring States period in China (403-221 BCE), and then in forms of Buddhism that were influenced by these writings, initially in Chan Buddhism in China in the second half of the first millennium CE and then in the Zen tradition which developed in Japan. (I shall be looking at the relation of this 'vision' to some forms of what we call 'religion' in the next chapter, asking whether it is, in some way, implicit there). I can claim no expertise in these areas and am dependent on translations of the primary texts, so what follows is not intended as a contribution to Daoist or Zen scholarship. Rather, I want to read these texts to further my articulation of this 'vision' since they emphasize and concentrate on aspects which I have not so far sufficiently explored. I shall first attempt an exposition of these aspects in the Daoist texts and in the writings of the Zen master Dogen (1200-1253 CE), and then try to bring together their common themes.

1.

'The Dao that can be told is not the constant Dao' (*Reading the Dao*, Keping Wang, London 2011, p. 141).
'The pursuit of learning is to increase day after day.
The pursuit of the Dao is to decrease day after day.
It decreases and decreases again.
Till one gets to the point of take-no-action (*wu-wei*).

He takes no action and yet nothing is left undone'. (*Dao De Jing* 48, Keping Wang *Reading the Dao*, London 2011, p. 160, hereafter Wang).

'Dao' as a nominative term is usually translated as 'way' but can relatedly mean path, method, teachings, and so forth (*Dao De Jing*, translated with commentary, R.T.Ames and D.L.Hall,, New York 2003, p. 57. Hereafter Ames and Hall.) As David Cooper remarks 'Talk of ways or courses for human beings to follow is pervasive in classical Chinese texts. A way was usually a human practice-fishing, say, or governing a country- as it ought to be, a practice skillfully conducted' (David Cooper, *Convergence with Nature*, Totnes, 2011, p. 58). Such 'ways' can be taught and so articulated to a certain degree: they would count as 'the pursuit of learning' and clearly increase the capacities of the learner. But Dao used as a stand alone term, indicated in the translations by the use of the definite article which is absent in Chinese, and so not the dao of a practice, cannot be articulated or taught. The first line of the *Dao De Jing* makes this clear:

'The Dao that can be told is not the constant Dao.
The Name that can be named is not the constant Name'
(Wang, p. 141).

This is emphasized in two other central Daoist texts. The *Nei-yeh* (Inward Training) tells us:

As for the Way:
It is what the mouth cannot speak of,
The eye cannot see,
And the ears cannot hear' (section 6, H.D.Roth, *Original Tao*, New York, 1999, p. 56, hereafter Roth.)

Dao, as a stand alone term, marks *mystery* as the *Chuang-tzu* emphasizes:

'Look it has no shape,
Listen, it has no sound.
In the discourse of men
It is called the mystery'. (A.C.Graham, *Chuang-tzu, The Inner Chapters*, Indianapolis, 2001, p. 162. Hereafter Graham).

We need above all to respect this rejection of articulating Dao and recognize that 'Dao' here is not a name, in the way the dao of fishing is. Rather, it has its sense in the context of 'the pursuit of Dao', as the *Chuang-tzu* says: ' 'Way' as a name is what we borrow to walk it' (Graham, p. 153). This pursuit is 'to decrease day after day': it is an 'inward training' that is a coming to a self-knowledge. This knowledge is not an 'increase', but rather a recovery of what has been covered over in ordinary life. And what we recover is the mystery which our lives are. But this is at the same time the uncovering of the mystery of the 'world' which, in our ordinary understanding, we take to be 'other' than ourselves:

'Venture not beyond your doors to know the world;
Peer not outside your window to know …(dao)' (Ames and Hall p. 150, *Dao De Jing* 47).

Dao, the mystery, 'abides within the excellent mind' and 'is not distant from us' (*Nei-yeh* 5, Roth p. 54), and coming to realize this is to come to realize the mystery of the world. Knowing Dao is knowing oneself and the world at the same time. In this way, the 'pursuit of dao' is the recovery of 'oneness':' The sages grasp oneness' (Ames and Hall p.110, *Dao De Jing* 22). The 'decrease day after day' is the loss of 'self' and 'other', of the duality which characterizes ordinary life in which a 'self' is formed through identification with goals pursued through the utilization of 'objects' selected out of an environment of 'otherness'. We 'walk' Dao in 'dropping off' self and other and in doing so we recover the *primordial* condition of life. Non-duality, the 'oneness' of life and world, is the presupposition for the separation of self and other. We always are already in the world and with others in non-duality. We need to recover an apprehension of this and thereby Dao as the mystery will become apparent: non-duality is realized as the mystery. In creating 'the self', pursuing our goals in the 'world' of otherness, life and the world constantly 'arise': 'Surging forth! It arises with us', 'Daily we make use of its inner power' (*Nei-yeh* 4, Roth p. 52). Without this constant unfolding there would be nothing to 'objectify' and no 'self' to think of. Non-duality is presupposed by the project of self and its attendant conceptions of 'object' and 'otherness', and is hidden by them:

'It is lost
Inevitably because of sorrow, happiness, joy, anger, desire and profit-seeking.
If you are able to cast off sorrow, happiness, joy, anger, desire, and profit-seeking
Your mind will revert to equanimity.
The true condition of the mind' (*Nei-yeh* 3, Roth p. 50).

A meditative practice, the details of which are unclear, was central in early Daoist circles in explicitly recovering non-duality. Roth quotes the *Chuang-tzu*:

'Unify your attention. Do not listen with the ears, listen with the mind. Do not listen with the mind, listen with the vital breath. The ears only listen to sounds. The mind is only aware of its objects. But to focus on the vital breath is to be empty and await the arising of objects. It is only the Way that settles in emptiness' (Roth pp. 154-5). But the point of this recovery is to *live* in accordance with Dao, in accordance with the mystery which non-duality, the arising of life and world, is.

Non-dual life is apprehended through 'dropping-off' the attachments to the temporal which are the result of forming a 'self' through identification with certain goals. Through that identification we have 'likes and dislikes', we live a life of discrimination, welcoming and rejecting. Through this dropping off, the 'myriad things' are manifest as they 'are', prior to the objectification and discriminating preferences of the 'self' pursuing its formation:

'When a properly aligned mind resides within you

The myriad things will be seen in their proper perspective' (*Nei-yeh* 10, trans. by Bruce R. Linnell, 2011, at www.gutenberg. org/files/38585/38585-pdf/38585-pdf.pdf).

Where 'self' and 'other' drop away, in the recovery of non-duality, Dao, the mystery, is manifest. The' myriad things' appear in their 'proper perspective' as 'given', beyond the objectification and discrimination of human beings, but as given *in* life which itself appears as 'arising'. In recovering non-duality, we realize the mystery of the giving of life and world, Dao.

We can see now why 'Dao' is the term used to point to the mystery: it is that which must inform the dao of human life, the way which characterizes the life of the Daoist sage:

'Those of magnificent character (*dé*)
Are committed to (Dao) alone' (*Dao De Jing* 21, Ames and Hall, p. 107).

That life will be one which in all aspects recognizes the priority of the mystery of the giving of life and world. And we can see too what it is that prompts the 'pursuit of Dao'. Ordinary life is characterized by the duality of self and world. But this duality follows from an internal duality in life. Dualistic life, the formation of a 'self,' not only poses the 'self' against the world, but life against itself. I, the living I which is life itself (it is always in the first person) objectifies the I as a 'self' to be achieved in the 'future' through identifying with certain goals, the 'real self'. This is illusory, since whatever is achieved, the living I still lives, and the future will remain as a projected 'self' always out of reach. The formation of 'self' is an expression of disharmony, of alienation from living life. This disharmony disappears with leaving behind dualistic life, in recovering the 'oneness' of life with itself and with the world. And that 'oneness' is revealed as formed through Dao, the mystery which is non-dualistic life. The sage 'will unify his nature' (Graham, p. 137) and in so doing will unify with 'the myriad things': 'The 'world' is that in which the myriad things are one. If you grasp the whole where they are one and assimilate yourself to it, ...nothing will be able to disturb you, least of all the distinctions drawn by gain and loss, good fortune and ill' (Graham, p. 131). So what is the way of one who follows Dao alone?

The first line of the *Dao De Jing*, 'The Dao that can be told is not the constant dao' suggests that there are ways that can be 'told' but constant Dao is not among them. It is, however, to such ways that the *Chuang-tzu* has recourse in order to provide insight into lives dedicated to constant dao alone. In the chapter 'What matters in the nurture of life' we are introduced to Cook Ting who is carving an ox for Lord Wen-Hui. Wen-Hui is impressed by Cook Ting's performance, remarking 'Oh, excellent. That skill should attain such heights',(Graham, *The Inner Chapters*, p.63). But Ting rejects this characterization: 'What your servant cares about is the Way, I have left skill behind me'. Now, 'I rely on Heaven's structuring ...(and) go by what is inherently so ...Whenever I come to something intricate, I see where it will be hard to handle and cautiously prepare myself, my gaze settles on it, action slows down for it, you scarcely see the flick of the chopper-and at one stroke the tangle has been unravelled'. Lord Wen-Hui remarks: 'Listening to the words of Cook Ting, I have learned from them how to nurture life'.

Again, in the chapter 'The advantages of Spontaneity', Duke Huan is reading, out of a concern with the Way, a book containing the words of a sage. A wheelwright remarks to the Duke that he is reading 'the dregs of men of old'. Duke Huan is incensed that a wheelwright should have the temerity to criticize what he is reading and demands an explanation or the wheelwright will die. The wheelwright says: 'Speaking for myself, I see it in terms of my own work. If I chip at a wheel too slowly, the chisel slides and does not grip; if too fast, it jams and catches in the wood. Not too slow, not too fast; I feel it in the hand and respond from the heart (the seat of understanding), the mouth cannot put it into words, there is a knack in it somewhere which I cannot convey to my son and which my son cannot learn from me. This is how through my seventy years I have grown old chipping at wheels. The men of old and their untransmittable message are dead. Then what my lord is reading is the dregs of the men of old, isn't it?' (Graham, pp 139-140).

The Cook and the wheelwright, at least in their capacity as butcher and carpenter, are in accordance with the constant way. Carving an ox and making a wheel are ways which can initially be articulated and taught and must be so for the cook and wheelwright to pass beyond what can so be articulated and taught. Through their heightened capacity, they see their situation in a way which cannot be expressed and their actions flow from this perception. This 'flow' of action from such perception of one's situation is 'spontaneity', ziran. Ziran means literally 'self-so-ing' or 'self-deriving' (Ames and Hall, p. 68) and is often translated as 'by nature', as when the activities of a squirrel flow spontaneously, in accordance with its nature as a squirrel. Carving and making wheels have been taken up into Cook Ting's and the wheelwright's 'nature' and their actions flow spontaneously from how, having that nature, they see their situations. They are at 'one' with the flow of activity (rather than, when one is at a lesser stage, trying to conform to a standard which is separate from oneself). And their being one with the flow of activity is being at one with what manifests itself in that flow. They spontaneously apprehend and respond to what manifests itself. Lord Wen-Hui says he has learned from Cook Ting's world 'how to nurture life': he has been given an insight into 'living according to Dao' in that Cook Ting's example points him towards the nature of non-dualistic life, albeit in the restricted exemplification in one particular 'way' of butchery. Although Cook Ting's and the wheelwright's activities are obviously concerned with production, they are not related to their activities as a means to further their 'life goals'. The activities have been taken up into their 'natures' so that they do what they do as expressions of themselves: in that sense, they do it 'for its own sake'. And such activity in its spontaneous flow is an open responsiveness to what manifests itself there. In this way, they are at one with life (in these particular forms) and with the world. Their activity *is* a non-dualistic manifestation of life and world, the mysterious giving of life and world which is constant Dao. The sage, however, *lives* in accordance with constant Dao, not merely in some particular activity. Such a life manifests non-duality: life at one with itself and with the world through receiving them as constantly given.

The inexpressibility of such perception is not, of course, divorced from language. Cook Ting's and the wheelwright's perception of their situations and the actions which flow from it are possible only in terms of the practices of carving and making wheels within which is embedded the appropriate forms of language. The way of the sage, although it passes beyond what can be taught and 'told', is the way of a linguistic being, unlike that of an animal. But the nature of the sage's language is other than that of the ordinary human living a dualistic life. The *Chuang-tzu* says the sage 'has the shape of a man' but 'is without what is essentially man' (Graham, p. 82). By 'the essentials of man' Chuang-tzu means 'Judging 'That's it, that's not it'', which he calls 'deeming'. 'Deeming' is the nature of the perspective of the ordinary person who lives the life of the 'self', the dualistic perspective of one who pursues temporal goals with which they identify and sees the world as a field of 'objects' to be controlled as a means to their ends. In such a perspective, the world appears in terms of approval, rejection or indifference, 'likes and dislikes'. It is this which is expressed in 'deeming'. Because the individual lives as a project of 'self-formation', they impose themselves on the world, seeing it in terms of their own self-projection. The sage lacks 'the essentials of man' in not pursuing a sense of 'self', seeing the world as an 'other' to be imposed on. The sage 'does not wound his person by likes and dislikes' but 'constantly goes by the spontaneous and does not add to the process of life' (Graham, p. 82). The sage does not impose the discriminations of the 'self' on the world but is 'selfless', receptive to the spontaneous giving of life and world, of the 'process of life', which is constant Dao. His utterances have the character of "spillover" sayings: "Spillover' saying is new every day' (Graham, p. 107). Graham tells us that this is so called after a kind of vessel which is designed to right itself when filled too near the brim (Graham, p.107 footnote). It is the utterance of someone whose life manifests a fundamental openness, a receptivity, a deference to the giving of life and world. The sage "In saying he says nothing'. If in saying you say nothing, all your life you say without saying, all your life you refuse to say without ever failing to say' (Graham, p. 107). This 'saying nothing' is not muteism: it is saying, the use of language, of one whose life, being dedicated to constant Dao, is characterized by the '*wu*' forms (Ames and Hall, p. 36).

'*Wu*' in general means 'no' or 'not'. The most famous of the Daoist *wu* forms is *wu-wei*, 'non-action'. As Chuang-tzu remarks, 'The doer of the Way everyday does less and less, less and less until he does nothing at all, and in doing nothing, there is nothing he does not do' (p;159). '*Wu-wei*' is not an absence of activity. On the contrary, those who follow Dao 'know how to work but not how to store, and give without thought of return' (Graham, p. 173). Their activity is, like the giving of Dao, 'for nothing', it is living life for itself, a life which is at one with the world, as revealing 'the myriad things'. Their activities are not part of the project of forming a 'self' and so oriented towards control and mastery of what is 'other' to that self. Rather, it is activity as celebratory of life and the world as given, as proceeding out of mystery and so as ever open and receptive to what may manifest itself. It is non-action in the sense of self-less, non-dualistic activity done for itself as revelatory of the world. It is not the 'action' of a 'self' on the world, imposing itself, but an expression of the 'oneness' of life and the world through a relation to constant Dao, the mystery of the giving of life and world. It is characterized by 'spontaneity', *ziran*, which is the nature of Dao. It is life lived, as the giving of Dao, for 'nothing', for itself. And such life is, as at one with the world, characterized by openness and responding spontaneously to what may manifest itself. 'Spill-over' saying is the language appropriate to such a life, a language expressive of an intimacy with a world which is ever manifest in changing ways. The *Chuang-tzu* calls such a life 'roaming'. The sages of old roamed 'in the emptiness where one rambles without destination …To ramble without destination is Doing Nothing (*wu-wei*)' (Graham, p. 130). One rambles without destination in living life for itself, without a goal, celebrating its intimacy with the world in being how 'the myriad things' can manifest themselves in their emergence out of mystery. Chuang-tzu encourages us to 'roam out into the infinite …In describing and sorting out shapes and bodies, remain joined with them in ultimate sameness. In ultimate sameness you have no self, and without a self from where would you get to have anything?' (Graham. P. 150). The dualistic life of self-formation is the life of acquisition, accumulation and control of the 'other'. Life as 'roaming' is celebration of life in its intimacy with the world.

The *wu* forms are, then, terms which characterize such self less celebratory life. *Wu-ming*, 'no-name', is naming, not as a constituent in a project of mastery and control of what is named in terms of ones 'likes and dislikes', but as a receptive recognition of what is given and openness to change. As with all the *wu* forms, it marks a receptivity, a deference, which is ever open to new revelation. *Wu-yu*, 'no-desire', is the desire, the affectivity, which characterizes the life of *wu-wei*. It is desire without an object, as celebratory of non-dual life, the desire to express this in various ways. It issues naturally in the music, poetry and art the sage is often depicted as enjoying, but equally in the enjoyment of simple, necessary tasks where, as with Cook Ting and the wheelwright, such activities are done for themselves. Similarly, *wu-zhi*, 'no-knowing', is understanding informed, not by a desire to control and master the world, but by a receptive openness to what may become manifest. It is knowing which does not 'store' but which is ever responsive to change.

The sage is 'dedicated to Dao alone' and so lives the non-duality which is the 'process of life' as 'given': the sage adds nothing to the process of life since he does not live as projecting a 'self' on it. In this dedication, the sage lives in a temporality other than that of the dualistic self. In the *Chuang-tzu*, the woman Chu expounds how one enters into non-duality. The aspiring sage must 'put the world outside him' (the world of 'objects' the 'self' orients itself towards to further its project), 'put the things we live on outside him' (the particular things the self 'likes' in seeing the world from the point of view of its self-formation), and then 'put life itself outside him' (the sense of 'self' itself). 'Once he had got life itself outside him, he could see …the Unique, and then he could be without past and present, and then he could enter the undying, unliving' (Graham, p. 87). The sage lives in terms of Dao, the timeless source of the flow of life in which the 'myriad things' presence. He lives in the timeless present of the giving of Dao. As the *Chuang-tzu* says, 'For the sage, there has never yet begun to be Heaven, never yet begun to be man, never yet begun to be a beginning, never yet begun to be things' (Graham, p. 111). The timeless present is 'uncovered' in the 'dropping off' of the hindrances the woman Chu identifies in breathing meditation: 'to focus on the vital breath is to be empty and await the arising of objects. It is only the Way that settles in emptiness. Emptiness is the fasting of mind' (Roth, p. 155, translation of *Chuang-tzu* chapter 4). The dualistic self lives in the future, looking towards the formation of its 'self'. In projecting the future, the 'self' leaves behind the past and utilizes objects the activities with which they identify reveal. Past, present and future are here relative terms, having sense only in relation to each other. But the 'present' of the sage is the timeless present of the 'process of life' itself. The living process of life is always in the *first* person. And it is this which marks the disharmony of the dualistic 'self' which prompts the reflection on life which may then result in the pursuit of dao, directed towards a recovery of harmony, of 'oneness'. Dualistically, 'I' project a 'self', and so am divided against myself. Dualistic life covers over the living present which is the presupposition for the projection of 'self' at all. This 'I' is not a 'self' but the timeless present which is the giving of life

and world. The point is to recover this, to live as 'I', and to live the
timeless present, or to live *timelessly*. To do so is to live life and the
world as constantly given, in terms of 'constant Dao'.

The sage who lives in terms of Dao is a person of 'superior
De'. 'De', often translated as 'power' or 'virtue', is a term like the
Greek *arête* which indicates the characteristics of a thing, plant,
animal or human which enables them to be an excellent one of
their kind. The 'excellent' human being is one who lives in terms
of Dao. So what are the characteristics of such a person? To live
in terms of Dao is to be at one with oneself and with the 'myriad
things' through fully recognizing that life is a revelation of the
'myriad things' and that this life is *given*. As the *Chuang-tzu* quotes
'heaven and earth were born together with me, the myriad things
and I are one', while cautioning that this cannot be regarded as
a statement which would imply a separation of the speaker from
the 'one' of which he is claiming to be part (*Chuang-tzu*, p. 56). It
is rather a 'reminder', a remark directed to recall the reader to
themselves, to the way they primordially are, the non-dualistic
living 'I' which is at one with 'myriad things'. To be at one with
oneself is to have no 'self' which one is trying to achieve through
pursuing goals. It is to live one's life as a constant gift and so not
in terms of an orientation to the future but *in* the present. It is in
that sense celebratory of life. But at the same time, being lived as
a gift, the sage does not 'choose' which would imply a separation
of self from the lived life of the present. Hence the *Chuang-tzu* says:

'Lighthearted! Seems to be doing as he pleases;
Under compulsion! Inevitable that he does it' (p. 85).

Receiving life out of mystery, Dao, as revelatory of the 'myriad
things', the sage's life is characterized by a fundamental receptivity,
a deference to the 'giving' which is Dao. The *Dao De Jing* (chapters
15 and 22) indicates certain fundamental characteristics of the
sage which follow from this. He is 'cautious and vigilant' (Wang),
responsive to what manifests itself, wary of imposing himself and
seeing things in terms of 'likes and dislikes'. He is 'solemn and

reserved' (Wang, 'dignified' Ames and Hall) 'as an invited guest', since he understands his life as the constant giving of Dao of which he is a 'guest'. He is 'supple and pliant' (Wang, 'yielding' Ames and Hall) since he is ever responsive to what may be given and so ever open to changing in thought, word and deed. He does not cling to his ideas and so sees things clearly (chapter 22) since to see them clearly is to recognize their givenness and his own receptive, passive stance. He is 'Genuine and plain, like the uncarved block' (Wang, 'so solid, like unworked wood' Ames and Hall).The 'uncarved block' is a metaphor for the primordial way life and the world are given together before being 'carved' by separation into 'self' and the 'other' of the field of objects for utilization in pursuit of the self's goals. He is 'Open and expansive' (Wang, 'vast and vacant' Ames and Hall) since he is ever open to what is given in a stance which embraces the 'whole'. He is 'merged and indifferent' (Wang) as at one with himself and the 'myriad things' and so not having 'likes and dislikes' which determine how he views things.

Receiving life and the 'myriad things' as they manifest themselves in human living involves recognizing that this is the giving of a 'human perspective'. Other forms of life too are given and there the 'myriad things' may manifest themselves in ways other than to us. Various passages in the texts refer to the different perspectives of animal forms of life (*Chuang-tzu*, pp 58, 204-5, for example). The sage will recognize the integrity and otherness of other beings, that they are not given for our exploitation in terms of our 'likes and dislikes'. (Although the sage is sometimes shown fishing and the domestication of animals in small farms which attends to their needs is recognized).

All this is about 'how' the sage conducts their life. But what do they do? One who 'walks the Way', like any other, finds themselves with a certain range of talents and abilities and within a given range of cultural possibiities. They are subject too to the necessity of maintaining themselves and their families. As the examples in the texts show, the follower of Dao may well engage in productive crafts directed toward making things useful for a life which recognizes itself as 'given'. Cook Ting, the wheelmaker, and the maker of bellstands (*Chuang-tzu*, p. 135) practise crafts useful to the maintenance and celebration of such life. Activities which address the 'likes and dislikes' of the 'self' in pursuing its ambitions and desire to stand out from others will not, however, form part of the sage's life. In engaging with crafts, one who is 'on the way' will utilize natural materials. Their relation to these emphasizes that they are 'given' and cannot be possessed:

> 'All under Heaven as a sacred vessel should not be acted upon Nor should it be held on to' (*Dao De Jing*, chapter 38, Wang).

Not to be 'acted upon' is not to pursue the goals of a 'self' but to take 'no action' (ibid.): to engage in the activity for itself in its capacity to reveal the 'myriad things' in a certain way. The account of the bellstand maker's approach to its making underscores this:

> 'I make sure to fast to still the heart. After fasting three days, I do not care to keep in mind congratulation and reward, honours and salary. After fasting five days, I do not care to keep in mind your blame or praise, my skill or clumsiness. After fasting seven days, I am so intent that I forget that I have a body and four limbs.
> ...The dexterity for it concentrates, outside distractions melt away, and only then do I go into the mountain forest and observe the nature of the wood as Heaven makes it grow. The aptitude of the body attains its peak, and only then do I have a complete vision of the bellstand, only then do I put my hand to it. Otherwise I give the whole thing up. So I just join what is Heaven's to what is Heaven's' (*Chuang-tzu*, p. 135).

No doubt the account is exaggerated to emphasize the primary point, that in order to engage in the activity in accordance with Dao, one must divest oneself of any ulterior purpose the 'self' might propose and indeed of any concern other than that for the activity itself: to prepare oneself to act simply for itself and so 'do nothing'. Only so will one's 'aptitude' be attuned in the right way

and only so will one 'see' both what is to be produced (something
not subject to the dictates of mere 'likes and dislikes') and the
nature of the wood. Only when we are 'without a self' (*Chuang-tzu*,
p. 51) do we see things as they are, as 'given', and so can see what
is to be produced and what is to be used in the right way.

Being 'one' with all things through Dao, the follower of the
way is 'one' with their fellow humans. Lacking a concern for 'self',
their relation to others is non-competitive, unaffected by issues
of power and status. Receiving life as a gift, their actions and
activities are themselves characterized by *wu-wei*, action which is
a giving 'for nothing'.

'The sage does not accumulate for himself.
The more he shares with others, the more he possesses.
The more he gives to others, the richer he becomes' (*Dao De
Jing*, chapter 77, Wang).

They are, therefore, compassionate, and, as 'He does not cling to
his ideas' and 'does not claim to be always right' (*Dao De Jing, chapter
22, Wang),* they are open and respectful of others. The one who is
' on the way' is concerned with the cultivation of 'profound De',
with following Dao, so that their lives have an essentially 'internal'
focus. As the *Chuang-tzu* puts it: 'When the sage sets in order, is the
ordering the external? It is simply a matter of straightening oneself
out before one acts, of being solidly capable of doing one's own work'
(Graham, p. 95). The sage is, therefore, uninterested in the world
of the pursuit of power, status and success. On being asked 'how
one rules the Empire', the 'man without a name' explodes: 'Away!
You're a bumpkin! What a dreary thing to talk about! I am just in
the course of being fellow man with the maker of things …What
do you mean by stirring up thoughts in my heart about such a trifle
as ruling the Empire? Let your heart roam in the flavourless, blend
your energy with the featureless, in the spontaneity of your accord
with other things, leave no room for selfishness, and the Empire
will be in order' (Graham, p. 95). Following the way is what matters
and only 'order' in human life which is in accordance with it is

worthwhile. Let all follow Dao and the Empire will look after itself.

2.

Dogen's Zen: 'When timelessness is realized, you are alive' (*Essential Dogen,* ed. Kazuaki Tanahashi and Peter Levitt, Boston 2013, p. 94).
'Zen is a practice of awakening. Who does one awaken as? What does one awaken to? The answers to both these questions is, in a word, 'emptiness'(Skt. *Sunyata,* Ch. *Kung,* Jp *ku*)'. (Bret W Davis, 'Forms of Emptiness in Zen' in *A Companion to Buddhist Philosophy,* John Wiley and Sons, 2013, p. 190).

It might seem natural to ask what 'emptiness' is and what are the arguments for taking it as central in determining the significance of life, which, if one found them persuasive, might lead one to aspire to 'awakening' oneself. However, this very 'naturalness' proceeds from an understanding of life and the world *from* which one 'awakens' in the practice of Zen. Such awakening is to the delusion of understanding oneself as a subject addressing in thought and action a world, including other subjects, separate from oneself, an understanding characterized as that of 'discriminating mind'. Not only does this understanding see the subject separated from the world but, more crucially, from itself. In this understanding I see my life as an issue to be resolved by determining some pattern of life as its solution: I find myself (here and now) unsatisfactory when judged from the position of a future I. In this way I am divided from myself. This division is the source of all unsatisfactoriness, *dukkha*, 'suffering', of life to which the Buddha's 'four noble truths', formulated in his first sermon after enlightenment, refer: all is suffering, there is an origin of suffering, there is a cessation of suffering, and there is a way leading to this cessation. However these 'truths' may have been understood in early Buddhism, within Zen the source of unsatisfactoriness lies in 'dualistic' thought and life in which I am separated from myself and from that world within which I am to look to resolve the issue of my life. 'Awakening' is a realization of the illusory nature of this 'duality' if that is taken as 'reality', as it is in ordinary purposive life and in the philosophies which articulate this 'natural' position. This awakening, 'realization', is a self realization in which the 'self' of the discriminating mind disappears. This radically affects how we are to hear formulations of the four 'truths' or of 'all things are empty'. We cannot understand these as claims about an issue ('the nature of the human condition') which would involve precisely the 'discriminating mind' the delusion of which we are awakening from. They are not statements about an issue the subject is addressing. 'The human condition' is not something I am separate from: 'addressing' it is 'addressing' myself. The formulations are rather expressions of this awakening, of non-dual apprehension. 'Emptiness' has then to be understood in this context: it is how things are manifest in non-duality. As I am going to say something about this, it might then be rejoined, surely this discussion is itself complicit in 'discriminating mind'. I am taking non-duality and how things appear non-dually as 'objects' of discussion and surely I will be stating certain things about them, claiming their 'truth', which others may dispute. This is indeed so, but here 'discriminating mind' is being used to discuss texts whose nature is to recall us to the dependency of 'discriminating mind' on non-duality. The 'delusion' of 'discriminating mind' lies in its claim to determine reality, in its failure, as we shall see, to understand itself as dependent on 'non-duality'. That we can, and indeed to an extent must, understand ourselves as purposive agents, and the world as a field within which purposes can be carried out, is not denied. What we awake to is that reality does not primordially manifest in this way, and when we do awaken to this our life itself takes on a different significance.

In 'awakening' the self of 'discriminating mind' falls away. 'To study the way of enlightenment is to study the self. To study the self is to forget the self. To forget the self is to be actualized by myriad beings. When actualized by myriad beings, your body and mind as well as the bodies and minds of others drop away. No trace of enlightenment remains and this no trace continues endlessly' (*The*

Essential Dogen, edited by Kazuaki Tanahashi and Peter Levitt, Boston and London 2013, p.53, hereafter *ED*). In realization, I and others as subjects and the world as a world of objects 'drop away', as too does 'enlightenment' as something aspired to. What drops away is the whole viewpoint of 'discriminating mind'. When the self is forgotten, so too are the 'myriad beings' as objects for the self to be thought, addressed, manipulated and so forth. Forgetting the self, the 'myriad beings' manifest themselves as they *are*, in their 'thusness', that is, as prior to their appearance as 'objects' for a subject. This is not a conception of them as 'things in themselves' beyond human understanding, but rather an emphasis that primordially human life *is* the manifesting of reality. Only so can 'discriminating mind' objectify what has already been *given*, or if that term sounds too anthropomorphic, what *manifests itself of itself.* There is self-manifestation of things in their 'thusness' which is at the same time the manifestation of the 'original face': 'You should stop searching for phrases and chasing after words. Take the backward step and turn the light inward. Your body-mind of itself will drop off and your original face will appear' (*ED*, p.5). The appearance of the 'original face' is just the manifestation of 'myriad things' in their thusness and this is 'non-duality'. 'To carry the self forward and illuminate myriad things is delusion. That myriad things come forth and illuminate the self is awakening' (*ED*, p. 55). 'Carrying the self forward' is the objectification of 'myriad things', in the furtherance of human control, intellectual and pragmatic. But there could be no 'subject' without the prior manifestation of the 'original face', nor 'objects' without the self-manifestation of 'myriad things' in their 'thusness'. 'Encountering the buddha face is nothing other than fully recognizing myriad things as myriad things' (*ED*, p.60). The 'buddha face' and 'buddha nature' are expressions for *self-manifestation*, of the self-arising of human life as the manifestation of reality. Dogen writes: 'all are buddha nature …know that the *are* of *all are buddha nature* is beyond are and are not. *All are* are the Buddha words, the Buddha tongue' (*Enlightenment Unfolds*, ed.Kazuaki Tanahashi, Boston and London 1999, p. 59). This 'are' points to the self-manifestation which is prior to our determination of something as existing or not, that is, taking it as an object of thought or judgement. But further, this 'are' of the 'buddha tongue' is itself a manifestation of the buddha tongue: 'all are Buddha nature' is the expression of a realization which *arises of itself.* 'Realization' is something which 'happens', it is not something we 'do', although we can open ourselves to the possibility of its advent. 'Are' and 'are not' are utterances of the 'discriminating mind', in which the subject affirms or denies what is in the world. The 'are' of the buddha tongue speaks out of non-duality, out of realization, awakening. It is beyond self and object since they can arise only out of a primordial non-duality. Hence terms like 'buddha nature' and 'emptiness' have to be understood in the context of realization, of non-duality. They are not terms which function in statements by a subject about 'the nature of reality', which would presuppose the separation of 'discriminating mind' from the object of its thought. They function either as expressions of realization or, said to another (as Dogen is doing), as prompts for self-recognition, as 'useful means', interventions to prompt the 'backward step', to 'turn the light inward'. Such formulations have an essentially negative character: 'emptiness' (of self and object, saying, as it were, not-self, not-object), non-self (anatman, Skr.), no-mind, buddha nature (not the nature the self projects). They are terms used not in assertions, but in intervening in the world of self and object in order to prompt a realization, a self-recognition, an awakening from the delusion of that world as 'reality'.

Such interventions can take forms other than apparent 'statements'. Those who 'seeking enlightenment' and so understanding themselves as subjects pursuing a goal about which they require knowledge of the relevant means, are frustrated by being presented with 'questions' which cannot be answered (the famous 'what is the sound of one hand clapping?' and similar '*koans*'). Or they are presented with accounts of Buddha ancestors who deny knowledge in situations where the answer seems obvious. Boddhidharma, who is said to have introduced the Zen tradition to China, was asked by the Emperor 'who is facing me?', and answered 'I don't know' (*EU*, p.140), a response which proceeds out of the 'dropping away of self'. The Emperor's question assumed an answer in terms of a 'subject', 'I', an assumption which Boddhidharma's response rejects. Again, at the first meeting between the sixth patriarch Hui-neng and Nan-yueh, the patriarch asked: 'Whence do you come?' 'I come from Tung-shan' 'What is it that thus comes?' Hui-neng asked. Nan-yueh did not know what to answer. For eight years he considered the question, then one day he had an insight and he exclaimed, 'Speaking about it won't hit the mark'. (*ED*, p. 48) The interrogative without an answer prompts a 'turn inward' from the world of the subject who expects an answer, a statement, in response to a question, towards a realization of the 'original face' which is the self manifesting of 'myriad things', towards an awakening to non-duality. Such a prompt can equally be given by occasions like David Cooper's 'epiphanies'. Realization is said to have been occasioned by a stone hitting bamboo (*EU*, p.61), through seeing peach blossoms in full bloom (*EU*, p.62), and Shakyamuni Buddha himself was enlightened by the morning star (*EU*, p.63). The tradition of Zen as a communication beyond scripture is traced back to the occasion on Vulture Peak when Shakyamuni Buddha held up an udumbara blossom and blinked. Mahakashyapa smiled, upon which the Buddha said 'I have the treasury of the true dharma eye, the wondrous heart of nirvana. I entrust it to Mahakashyapa'. Realization can be occasioned by the holding up of a flower. Indeed, as Dogen points out, in the right circumstances anything can be such an occasion: 'bring forth the turning point by using a finger, a pole, a needle, or a mallet, or leading people to enlightenment with a whisk, a fist, a stick, or a shout cannot be understood by discriminatory thinking' (*EU*, pp33-4).

Realization, enlightenment, cannot be thought of as a state of the self and 'aspiration for enlightenment' must be seen as delusion. Realization is the loss of the self and so the loss of enlightenment as a state of the self to which one might aspire. 'Enlightenment' itself must drop away: 'No trace of enlightenment remains and this no-trace continues endlessly' (*ED*, p. 53). The loss of the self is the loss of projections of the self on non-duality, and so the loss of all projects including that for enlightenment itself. As the *Heart Sutra* puts it: 'Therefore, given emptiness, there is …neither ignorance nor extinction of ignorance …no suffering, no cause (of suffering), no cessation (of suffering), no path, no knowledge and no attainment' (*Realizing Genjokoan,* Shohaku Okumura, Somerville, 2010, p. 205). In this way, the sutra opposes construing the 'four noble truths' as 'statements' to be grasped and justified. Rather, they are interventions in discriminatory life which can open the individual to non-duality. 'Realization is reality right now' (*ED,* p.97): it is being brought into *the living present* which is the self-manifestation of 'myriad things' and which is the presupposition for the possibility of having projects and purposes at all.

This self-manifestation of the 'original face' and 'myriad things' which constitutes non-duality is Buddha Nature. As such, it is 'impermanence': reality is not given once and for all ('creation') as a permanent settlement, but as constant self-manifestation. Dogen says: 'time itself is being and all being is time' (*ED,* p. 93). In 'discriminatory mind', the understanding of life in terms of a subject living in the world, time appears 'objectively', as moving from past to future through the present. The subject sees the past as gone, the future as still to come and the present as what currently confronts them. But, as Masao Abe asks (*A Study of Dogen,* Albany, 1992, p. 116), where do we stand when we understand time like this? Dogen points out 'Time is not separate from you, and as you are present, time does not go away' (*ED,* p. 92). This 'present' is not one relative to past and future, but the 'present' within which past, (relative) present and future can be manifest. It is the present of existing life which is the life of non-duality, how life primordially is. This 'present' is 'transtemporal', the 'absolute now', *nikon.* This is the 'time' of the self-manifesting of the 'original face' and the 'myriad things', of the presencing of reality. Such presencing is not relative to past and future and so this time is not marked by passing:'you are the time-being right now. This is the meaning of time-being (*uji*)' (*EU,* p. 71). *Nikon,* transtemporal presencing, is the self manifesting of the world in the manifesting of life. 'Since there is nothing but just this moment …Each moment is all being, is the entire world' (*EU*, p.70). Buddha nature can therefore be called 'time'.

Nikon is entered in *zazen*, the 'just sitting' meditation which Dogen saw, not as a means towards realization, but as realization itself: this is 'the practice-realization of complete enlightenment' (*EU*, p. 33). We 'sit steadfastly and think not-thinking. How do you think not-thinking? Beyond thinking. This is the essential act of *zazen*' (ibid.) 'Thinking' is by a subject about a matter. It is a manifestation of dual life. To *think* non-duality is still to think, to take non-duality as an object of thought. To enter non-duality is 'beyond thinking', to live in the permanent now, *nikon*, which is the self- manifesting of the original face as the self-manifesting of 'myriad things'. This is not 'thought', although its being 'beyond thinking' can be thought, just as enlightenment is said to be 'inexpressible' but its inexpressibility can be expressed.

'Emptiness' is not a word which can function in a statement. 'All things are empty' is, like Boddhidharma's 'I don't know' or Hui-neng's 'What is it that thus comes?', an intervention in everyday purposive life, a provocation to realization, that stops the temporal flow of that life in 'right now', *nikon*. 'Emptiness' is emptiness of duality, of the conceptuality derivative of subject and object, directing us to the 'reality' which is primordial and is the presupposition for the self and world of duality. It is in terms of this that we can understand the various uses of the term 'emptiness' that Bret Davis identifies.

All things are 'empty of own being'. Dogen writes: 'If you examine things with a confused body and mind, you might suppose that your mind and essence are permanent. When you practice intimately and return to where you are, it will be clear that nothing at all has unchanging self' (*EU*, p.36, *ED*, p. 53). In terms of 'discriminatory mind', the subject thinks and relates to a separate world of objects and so appears as the permanent substrate for thought and action. But when 'body and mind drop away' and non-duality manifests itself, you are 'intimate' with 'myriad things' and so there is no separation, the 'original face' is the self-manifestation of 'myriad things'. As there is no self, there are no objects, and as the 'original face' is the self-manifestation of 'myriad things' there is nothing (no thing) permanent. There is only the timeless present (*nikon*) of this manifestation in its constant change. Hence, 'Impermanence is the truth that is right in front of you' (*CD*, p. 31). All things are dependent on this self-manifestation and are interconnected as moments of it. 'The way the self arrays itself is the form of the entire world. See each thing in the entire world as a moment of time' (*ED*, p.92). When we realize beings as time (that is, their being as 'thusness' in the timeless present of *nikon*), we realize their impermanence and 'dependent origination' (Skt *pratitya samutpada*). We realize their being as 'thusness' and so as dependent on 'self-manifestation'. And in this realization, all beings are given, as self-manifestation is 'thusness'. So, although empty of 'own being', a being in its thusness is interconnected to all others. All being and all time is contained in the moment of realization.

Beings are manifest in their 'thusness' in realization: the pine tree, the bamboo 'just as it is', empty of human projections. At the same time, this is the manifestation of the 'true self', 'the original face': we are in our 'thusness', freed from the duality of self and other. Self-manifestation of 'myriad things' essentially involves us-we become enlightened, other beings attain enlightenment with our realization, in manifesting in their 'thusness'. Although 'buddha dharma ...is attained by letting go of the mind and abandoning views and interpretations', and is 'the teaching that is not concerned with concepts and theories' (*Beyond Thinking*, ed. Kazuaki Tanahashi, Boston 2004, pp 10, 14) realization is of *us*, as linguistic beings. The *pine* tree, the *bamboo* are manifest as they are: this is not a pointing to a 'thing in itself' beyond human capacities, but a revelation of the primordial way beings and ourselves are *pre-reflectively*, prior to the emergence of the separation of self and world. What manifests itself is ourselves in unreflective action which is the self manifestation of 'myriad things'. The pine tree manifests in its thusness, empty of human projections, but in a context which in its indeterminateness flows out encompassing 'all beings'. The pine tree appears in relation to earth, sky, sun and cloud and other plants and animals, and these themselves point to ever wider contexts, so that a 'whole', 'all being and all time' manifests itself. 'Dependent origination' points to this contextual nature of self manifestation. The pine tree in its 'thusness' is dependent on its connectivity to all else, and in this to self-manifestation itself, the arising, we might say, of the pine tree out of mystery.

Although for Dogen, sitting in *zazen* is non-duality, and so realization, enlightenment, the point is to *live* non-dually. In non-duality, the pine tree is 'just as it is': so non-dual life is life 'just as it is'. This is to live with 'no-mind', to live life freed from the imposition of the conceptuality and temporality of self and other. Life is not a project to be attained in mastering circumstances and discriminating others in relation to such a project. We might say that non-dual life is life lived 'for nothing', simply for itself. Although human life is purposive, means and ends have equal significance: one lives, not projected into the future, but in the existential present. It is this which reveals the delusion of 'seeking enlightenment'. Thomas Kasulis (*Zen Action Zen Person*, Hawaii, 1987, p. 41) relates the following exchange: 'Once a monk made a request of Joshu. 'I have just entered the monastery,' he said.

'Please give me instructions, Master'.

Joshu said, 'Have you had your breakfast?'

'Yes, I have,' replied the monk.

'Then', said Joshu, 'wash the bowls'. The monk had an insight'. The monk, thinking that he was embarked on a project, to gain enlightenment, requires information about how this is to be achieved. Joshu's response recalls the monk to the non-duality which is always already the character of life. In pursuing our projects, our eyes, as it were always on the future, in terms of the separation of self and other, reality, our own and of 'myriad things' continually unfolds in the existential present. We, of course, don't notice this as to do so would be to objectify what cannot be objectified. In this unfolding there is no separation: there is simply the presencing of the trees, bushes, sky and sun as we walk along. Our walking is the self manifesting of 'myriad things'. There is no 'I' and no 'other', and no time but the existential present. To live non-dually is to live in the existential present rather than the projected future which separates me from myself. It is that separation which is the origin of *dukkha*, unsatisfactoriness. To see life non-delusionally is to see, as Dogen says, there is only the existential now: 'When timelessness is realized, you are alive' (*ED*, p. 94). The timeless now, *nikon*, is the presencing of 'the original face' which is the manifesting of 'myriad beings'. We might say, although this involves an anthropomorphism, to live in the timeless now is to live life as a constant giving of ourselves and the world.

Dogen emphasizes in relation to *zazen* that practice and realization are one. It is not that one practices in order to achieve realization as a goal (of a subject for whom practice is a means). Rather, that dualistic understanding of 'practice' (action, thinking, human activity and so life) must 'drop away'. There is just practice which is realization, non-duality, living in the timeless present. There is no separation of self and other in relation to 'myriad things' or to myself as when I live oriented to the future. The practice is, we might say, wholly us, life at that moment. We have intimations of this in our purposive activities. We may be embarked on some intellectual project, like this one, but then it is no longer us thinking in order to achieve a goal, but rather the thinking is us. There is just the thinking: there is a passivity, a receptivity, which obliterates the separation involved in speaking of my thinking about an issue. When Dogen says of *zazen* we think not-thinking by non-thinking, he is pointing to this receptivity, this openness which characterizes living in the existential present, non-dual life. A musician becomes the music she is playing: she is not related to it as a task to be carried out, she is the presencing of the music. This can characterize listening to music too. One is no longer trying to follow the musical logic, to make sense of the piece, or daydreaming while it plays, but you and the music are one. You are the presencing of the music. We may say afterwards that you were 'lost in the music'. But this is an external viewpoint, separating you as subject from the music. The whole thrust of Zen is to recall us from the external viewpoint on our lives which is involved in living oriented to the future to living in the existential present, in the timeless now which is life. And that *is* the self manifestation of reality. It is non-dual life.

Realization is recall to what we are any way, 'since there is nothing but just this moment' (*EU*, p. 70), as Dogen says. 'The aspiration for enlightenment arouses itself …it is not limited by conditions' (*ED*, p.4). It arises in the self reflection occasioned by the dissatisfaction which is the nature of separate dualistic life because there I am separated from myself, living projected to a non-existent future. Where the issue or problem of 'the meaning of life' arises in that reflective turn, this is an expression of that dissatisfaction. The temptation here is to continue this separation by looking for a solution, some goal towards which I can direct my life. What is needed rather is the disappearance of the 'issue' in a recovery of the 'thusness' of myself so I am no longer separated from myself. This realization may arise in the confusion of the occurrence of 'the problem of life', but, of course, it may not. If it does, it is itself enlightenment, the self-manifesting of the delusion of dual life as delusion. But then, just as Dogen says to the beginning practitioner, 'Do not try to be a Buddha', so it would be delusion to then take non-dual life as a goal. Rather, non-duality as openness to what presences transforms me in the dropping away of 'mind and body', of the concerns of separate dual life, and then 'discriminatory mind' can be used in appropriate ways guided by the concerns of non-dual existence. Life as separation involves the pursuit of life goals, of taking some activities and relationships as central to my life but living them projected into the future. Nonduality transforms this life. Some projects fall away as incompatible with living in the timeless present: the pursuit of fame, status, money cannot be lived in the present as the pursuit is separate essentially from what gives the pursuit its point. To live in the present is for the activity, the relationship *now* to be the point. Other activities and relationships reveal their capacity for 'non-thinking', 'non-action', for living in the timeless present. Here they are lived for themselves, manifesting the 'thusness' of myself, others and 'myriad things. This is not something I can take as a goal without being deluded. What one can do is to open oneself to the possibility of being transformed, of being recalled to who you are.

3.

I can perhaps summarize the congruities important for the present inquiry found in the visions of Daoism and Zen in the following way.

1) The nature of the 'issue of life' to which 'enlightenment' or the 'life of the sage' are responses.

The life of the sage or that of enlightenment appears as a response to the reflective break in unreflective life where the issue of the measure for life arises, that in terms of which its meaningfulness is to be understood. This is likely to find expression in asking what form of life the individual is to take as a 'goal' to pursue in which they would become their 'true self', and in the pursuit of which the world beyond the 'I' is a field of 'useful', 'hostile' and 'indifferent' 'objects', a field of 'means' in relation to the goal. But this separation of 'self' and 'other' presupposes a fundamental unity in which life is the revealing of the world and in which there is no separation of the living 'I' from itself implied in aiming towards a future 'self'. That 'oneness' is the nature of the primordial way in which life and world are *given*. It is there we find the measure for life. Both Daoism and Zen emphasize that the life of the sage or that of enlightenment are not to be taken as 'goals'. The reflective break in unreflective life is precipitated by a disquiet, the origin of which lies in the separation of the living 'I' from itself in the pursuit of a 'self' and the resulting separation of life from world. This is the felt 'unsatisfactoriness', '*dukkha*', which, if its root is identified, can then motivate the move to 'drop away' 'self' and 'other' as the fundamental way in which one thinks about life. This is to return to the *living* 'I' which cannot be identified with a 'self' which can be taken as an 'object' to aim at. We find the measure for life by recovering the primordial way in which life and the world are given in the flow of everyday life, and so being returned to ourselves.

2) The recovery of the nature of unreflective life.

To return to the living 'I' is to drop away 'self' and so to drop away 'other'. It is to recover living life as the manifesting of 'myriad things', to recover the nature of the primordial way in which there is no separation from the world. The nature of unreflective life is revealed in this as the spontaneous arising of 'myriad things', which we then realize characterizes our everyday activities. Those activities are, of course, those of a linguistic being, so the 'arising' is of the 'bamboo', the 'pine tree', but without the categories of 'useful', 'obstacle', or 'indifferent', the result of the 'likes and dislikes ' of the discriminating 'self'. It is the arising of things as they 'are', in their self-emergence, as something 'given', arising mysteriously. The arising is of things in an environing context (it arises in *life*) which points ever beyond itself. The pine tree arises in relation to the earth, the sky, plants and animals, and so to ever wider contexts. The 'human world' arises in the arising of the pine tree or bamboo, and as 'arising' it points to other possible 'arisings' in the case of other sentient beings whose 'worlds' are other than our own.

3) The temporality of the 'giving' of life and world.

This arising of life and world, this 'giving', is the time of the living 'I', the 'timeless present' of *nikon* or the 'deathless'. This is the presupposition for the projection of a 'self' and conceiving of a world of objects. That understanding involves a separation of the 'I' from a past which is already done with, a future which is awaited and a present to be engaged with. But the 'I' is not separate from time: the 'I' is the living timeless present which is the arising of 'I' and world. In recovering the nature of unreflective life in this way, I see that the point is to live *in* the timeless present, not in a 'future' which is the projection of an illusory identification of the 'I' with a self. The 'present life' in no longer seen as a means to a future self, but is lived for itself. To 'drop away' the 'self' is to allow attachment to temporal goals to drop away. The life of the sage or of the enlightened is just this recovery of living life, of life as constantly arising ('given') in the arising of the world, 'myriad things'. It is the recovery of ourselves as we *are*, as given. We 'are' beyond 'likes and dislikes' in 'arising', in being 'given' out of mystery.

4) The negative language of the texts.

The language of the Daoist and Zen texts has to be heard within this context of 'dissolving' the 'problem' of life through dropping away the understanding of 'self' and 'other' which gives it rise. There is no Daoist or Zen 'doctrine' of the 'nature of the human condition' or of 'reality'. The sayings of these texts are rather 'reminders' to prompt us to a recollection of the primordial way in which we are, the living 'I', prior to the imposition of the notions of 'self' and 'other'. Their vocabulary is therefore essentially negative. 'Emptiness' (of the projections of 'self' and 'other'), 'non-self' (*anatman*), 'Buddha-nature' (not the nature projected by 'self' and 'other', of 'discriminating mind') in Zen, and the *wu* forms in Daoism: *wu-wei* (no-action, non-dual action which flows spontaneously (*ziran*) from life lived for itself), *wu-yu* (no-desire, the desire which characterizes life lived for itself, as 'arising', in accordance with Dao), and so forth. These terms are saying to us: not-self, not-other, no-goal, to recall us to the primordial way in which life and he world are given. There can equally be non-verbal interventions which prompt 'realization' and experiences we may undergo which can do this to (like David Cooper's 'epiphanies').

It remains to ask about the relation of such a 'vision of mystery' to what we call 'religion'. I will begin by returning to Kierkegaard to contrast his understanding of the 'issue' which the 'existing doubter' faces with that we have found in Daoism and Zen. I shall suggest that his understanding of Christianity as a response to this issue is incompatible with such a 'vision', before raising the question whether other forms of religion may be more hospitable.

Chapter 5

The Vision of Mystery and Religion.

1.

I began this inquiry with a reference to Kierkegaard's 'existential' critique of Hegel's, and by implication other philosophers', treatment of the issue of the 'Truth' in which to live. That is, that they treat this as an intellectual problem to be addressed in a disinterested spirit, which must be settled prior to any rational decision as to how to live, rather than as the profound existential disturbance it must be for a living individual. Kierkegaard accused philosophers of failing to fully recognize the implications of the obvious fact that they are human beings themselves, and that philosophical issues must be located within the context of living individual life, and the sort of response which is appropriate to them must be determined by what can address an issue so located. I suggested that Wittgenstein and Heidegger took Kierkegaard's strictures seriously and worked out what philosophical practice might then look like. But clearly my inquiry has led us to a very un-Kierkegaardian place and I want now to understand the nature and consequences of this disparity, which can lead to some reflections on the relation between the vision of 'mystery' and practices and beliefs we are familiar with as 'religious'.

Let me return to Kierkegaard's description of how the issue of 'the Truth' arises for the existing individual. 'The youth is an existing doubter; continually suspended in doubt, he grasps for the truth- so that he can exist in it …for the existing person pure thinking is a chimera when the truth is supposed to be the truth in which to exist' (*CUP*, p. 310). The youth is already an existing individual, living life unreflectively and so inhabiting some sense of the 'meaning' of their life when this unreflective flow is broken and the 'issue' arises. Her activities and relationships lose their significance so that the 'I' is separated from them and the question arises of what can give meaning to life lived by this 'I'. This break is, for Kierkegaard, the manifestation of freedom: the negative 'doubt' releases the separated 'I' who realizes she must 'choose choice itself' as Judge William in *Either/Or* puts it. What gives meaning to the life of the 'I' is the capacity for choice, for freedom, independent of any result. The individual is to take over the activities and relationships she was previously immersed in, or others which are culturally available, unconditionally, if they can be so willed. The unreflective basis from which freedom can emerge Kierkegaard calls the 'aesthetic' life, within which the 'I' is immersed in activities and relationships with which she identifies. For Kierkegaard, this failure to separate the 'I', to realize the individuality of life, is not only the basis from which individuality must arise, but characterizes what he calls 'paganism'. Socrates is credited with separating subjectivity from the substantiality, the actuality, of Greek life, although he did not then go on to develop the idea of a life of freedom (*The Concept of Irony*, trans. Hong and Hong, Indiana 1989, p. 176). The aesthetic life finds its meaning in immersion in, unreflective identification with, activities and relationships, in as Judge William puts it, 'enjoying life' (*Either/Or*, trans. Hong and Hong, 1987, p. 179). This failure to realize the 'I' in its freedom from available concrete forms of life is attachment to finitude. It is the base both individually and culturally from which the separation of the 'I' can occur. Humans naturally love finitude (*Journals*, trans Hong and Hong, 1967, 1823), Kierkegaard writes, and it is here that the human and earthly conceptions of good and evil, pleasant and unpleasant reside (*Journals*, 1509). Such aesthetic 'life views' see the significance of life as lying in the achievement or maintenance of certain finite conditions, in a spectrum from the simple egotism of seeing meaning in terms of individual accumulation, to the attachment to specific forms of life characterizing 'human' cultural value systems. The aesthetic is, Kierkegaard says, a 'relativism' since different people and peoples are attached to different conditions, Greek aristocrats to agonistic life, the struggle to excel and achieve glory (*kleos*), while others may be attached to what Nietzsche called the 'bovine' conditions of security, moderate prosperity and contentment. But there is in all such aesthetic lives a lack of self-knowledge. A life lived aesthetically would lose significance for the 'I' were the relevant finite conditions to cease to be available, either for the individual or more generally for a people's way of life. But the individual 'I' would still live. Those ways of life were lived by individuals, by the existing 'I', and this is not identical with the forms of life with which aesthetically the 'I' identified. Aesthetic life in its immersion, in its unreflective identification of the 'I' with certain finite conditions, is essentially a form of existential illusion. It is this which becomes manifest when Kierkegaard's youth becomes an 'existing doubter'.

Confronted with one's freedom from the content of one's life, one can either retreat in self-deception or 'choose choice itself'. The 'I' chooses the content of her life without reference to finite conditions and so undertakes timeless commitments. Her talents become the basis for vocation, her sexuality for marriage, and since her choices are unconditional, she accepts what may befall. This 'ethical' life is something we all can do, it is, Judge William says, the 'universal task'. But this universality is to be contrasted with the exceptional which characterizes the religious (*Journals* 4469). Here, in its first form, the individual 'I' is further distinguished from the finite, temporal world. The ethical life is lived in the world of family and work, its orientation is outwards, although a movement illuminated by the infinite. The religious movement is inward, concerned solely with emphasizing the separation of the 'I'. 'To die to the world means voluntarily to give up the things of the earth. This is Christianity' (*Journals*, 3768). The 'I' is separated from the world in a movement to 'infinitize' itself, to live solely in terms of the infinite or the eternal. The 'I' expresses this by actively severing its attachments to finite conditions, turning inward to master its inclinations to be affected in its life valuation by what happens in the world. The primacy of the infinite for the religious individual may therefore call for the violation of the commitments which characterize ethical life, an hypothesis pictured for us in *Fear and Trembling* by Abraham's intended sacrifice of Isaac. The ultimate separation of the 'I' from finitude would then be living fully in terms of the eternal, no longer actively 'dying to the world', where one's will would be God's will (the will which, outside the finite temporal world, 'creates'). This is not something the 'I' can undertake, but, if it is possible, must be granted by the eternal, God. This possibility is pointed to in the life of the 'knight of faith' in *Fear and Trembling*.

This throws into relief the character of Kierkegaard's criticism of Hegel and the philosophical tradition in relation to 'the Truth' in which to live. The philosophical tradition treats this as an 'objective' issue, to be addressed disinterestedly, one to be resolved in arriving at the final truth about the reality of life and the world as it any way is. But this is not a position available to any existing individual. However, one might say, such a position is indeed that of the eternal, of God. As Kierkegaard (or at least his pseudonym Johannes Climacus) remarks, criticizing Hegel's claim to arriving at the 'final' truth about reality in his 'system', 'A system of existence cannot be given. Is there, then not such a system? That is not at all the case. Neither is this implied in what has been said. Existence itself is a system-for God, but it cannot be a system for any existing spirit' (*CUP*, p. 118). Philosophy, in claiming to reveal the nature of reality and human life 'as it any way is', aspires after a position unavailable to any existing individual. But this doesn't mean there is no such position, that of 'eternity', and nor does it mean that human aspiration after it is misplaced. On the contrary, that aspiration must be followed in the only way available to an existing individual, by separating itself from the world in ethical choice, and then by dying to the world expressing the aspiration to live solely in terms of the eternal. Philosophy's aspiration must be converted into the existential aspiration of the 'I' to become solely 'I' through this movement, to be taken up completely by the eternal, God.

One can see here how Kierkegaard's response to the movement of reflection, the break in immersive unreflective life, of the 'existing doubter', has an opposite trajectory to that of Daoism and Zen, and of the line of philosophical inquiry we have followed. For them, the moment of existential reflection is the occasion for a recovery of ourselves by a deepened understanding of the unreflective way we are in the world. It is a reflective recovery of how we and the world are given together in the stream of life which is the living 'I'. The danger of the moment of reflection, that this living 'I' will objectify itself and so bring about a self-alienation, is precisely what Kierkegaard lauds. Kierkegaard's separate 'I' is always to be achieved by 'dropping away' the world, holding before itself the transformation into 'eternal life'. For Zen, the 'dropping away' is not of the world, but of the obstacles to a realization of the oneness of human life and the world in their givenness. The way of enlightenment is to forget the self, and so the opposition of self and other, to 'drop off' life understood in those terms.

For Kierkegaard, the transitions between unreflective aesthetic life (including its aesthetic 'ethical' forms which involve a reflective assertion of aesthetic attachment to the temporal), the religious ethical and the religious proper take place as 'leaps'. The movement from aesthetic immersion in the world to the religious ethical requires that one despairs over the aesthetic as such. Within aesthetic attachment, the significance of life is always dependent on what happens in the world. Life is, therefore, always subject to a potential loss of meaning. But if some relationship or project to which the individual is attached becomes impossible, the consequent despair is not over the aesthetic as such. For the aesthetic individual, renewed attachment elsewhere is the obvious solution to despair. Rejecting the aesthetic as such would make no sense, a cure worse than the disease. All we can say, Kierkegaard would suggest, is that such despair over the aesthetic may occur, revealing our freedom, which may then be seized upon giving a new form of meaning to life. A 'leap' into the ethical may occur.

If it does, it is not because the individual recognizes some hidden contradiction in aesthetic life which then prompts a move to a 'higher' form of existence, but because of the *external* attraction of the eternal. For Kierkegaard, the series of transitions (if it occurs) shows *the activity of the eternal, of God*. Within the aesthetic, the 'I' is always an actual or potential concrete 'I' identified by certain temporal conditions. The recognition of the 'I' as essentially separate conceptually from the world is a *revelation* not a self-recognition. Of course, to say this is to emphasize that Kierkegaard's description of the transitions does not take place from a disinterested standpoint. No such standpoint exists for the existing individual. Nietzsche, for example, would simply deny that an individual who claimed to be undertaking 'timeless' commitments revealed the attracting power of the 'eternal'. Rather, he would say, they exhibit attachment to temporal conditions as much as any life must, to security bred from a fear of the possible loss of meaning in life. Indeed, Nietzsche would see the whole sequence of 'life-views' culminating in Christianity as a progressive attempt by the individual to secure herself against all possibility of failure, as a craving for absolute security. This is as much a human craving as that for glory, but one which deludes itself as to its nature. For Nietzsche, the point is to recognize and live the human projection of value onto life and the world, not to pretend the responsibility for this lies elsewhere. I think Kierkegaard would have agreed that if we fully recognize that the thinker is herself a human being who cannot transcend the human condition to occupy a disinterested position, then any such account of spiritual or moral development is going to involve an engaged 'life-view'. For the Christian Kierkegaard, the transitions between life views exhibits the increasing presence of God, the eternal, in the individual's life, as the individual gradually realizes their absolute dependence on the eternal for the significance of the living 'I' in its separation from the temporal, from the finite world. For Nietzsche, they exhibit an increasingly neurotic desire for complete safety from what may occur.

Within the Daoist and Zen vision, the 'transitions' from

unreflective life to Enlightenment or the life of the sage is a process of self-understanding, a recovery of who we anyway are. Enlightenment or the life of the sage is not, then, a 'goal' for life to be attained by a 'self'. The point rather is to lose the perspective in which such a project could be expressed. The motivation for losing this perspective is precisely the separating of the living 'I' from itself which it involves, which is for Kierkegaard the very manifestation of freedom and its projection of the ethical self to be achieved. What for Kierkegaard shows the first activity of the eternal in drawing the individual towards God, is for the Daoist or Zennist an escalation of self-delusion. Whereas for Kierkegaard the ethical and religious categories prescribe new forms of life, and so are positive characterizations of those forms of life we are to take on, the terms of Daoism and Zen are negative, pointing to the losing of the separation of self and other. They are interventions in the life lived in terms of 'self' to open it to the possibility of recovery, prompting the 'backward step'. It is true that the recognition that the life of the 'self' involves an alienation from the living 'I', prompting the movement towards its loss, must be something that 'happens' within the flow of life. But that is itself a manifestation of the nature of the flow of life, that it is given. Its happening is itself a moment of self-recognition which can then prompt the development towards full realization of the living 'I'. For Dao and Zen, the issue is not becoming an 'I' separate from the world, but recognizing one's primordial unity with the world in their mutual givenness. The process is one of shedding illusions as to who one already is, a recovery of how one is *primordially* living in the world.

It may appear that the notion of the 'timeless' plays a pivotal role both in Kierkegaard and in Daoism and Zen. But the term has a differing sense in the two contexts. The 'eternal' in Kierkegaard is the measure for temporal life in being the position from which life and the world are subject to a 'Last Judgement', the determination of a 'final truth'. This is to project an 'external' position to life and the world from which they can be subject to judgement. Kierkegaard's argument with philosophy is that it assumes it can occupy such a position, which is impossible for an existing individual; it is not that such a position is inconceivable. Rather, it is to be held before oneself as an unattainable (by human means) aspiration, in terms of which one can only confess one's inadequacy by *asceticism*. Kierkegaard writes in the *Journals* (4057) 'asceticism is really the view of life that regards God as the unconditioned and believes that before God this world is immersed in evil, is a penitentiary, and asceticism voluntarily endeavors to express this idea of the world that God has'. The Daoist and Zen understanding is focused, not on an external point from which the flow of life is subject to a 'final judgement' (and so 'objectified'), but on the timeless point which is the living present which characterizes the flow of life. The unreflective life, what Kierkegaard calls the aesthetic, is indeed a life of attachment to temporal goals, and in this evidences already a separation of the 'I'. The dualistic self, the 'discriminating mind', lives in the future, oriented towards the formation of the 'self'. (This is, of course, exacerbated when in Kierkegaard the 'I' separates itself from the flow of life in an aspiration towards 'eternal life'). But the 'I' who looks towards the future self can do so only because the 'I' is the living timeless present. In Dogen this is *nikon*, the 'absolute now': 'the time right now is all there is'. In Chuang-tzu this is the 'undying' (Graham, p. 87). The sage or the enlightened *lives* in the timeless present explicitly: 'when timelessness is realized, you are alive' (*ED*, p. 94). This is the present of the giving of life and the world: it is the present of living life itself ('you are alive') and of the presencing of things ('Realization is reality right now' (*ED*, p. 97). The 'absolute now' or 'timelessness' is the very nature of living life itself. The point is to live this explicitly and not in a 'future' to which the 'present' and 'past' are relative terms. The 'absolute now', the living present, is rather that point from which it is possible to project a future, relate to a past, and confront things in a present. To turn away from the primacy of the future, to explicitly live in the 'absolute now', is to live without illusion.

Kierkegaard's Christianity is a 'revealed' religion according to which the measure for life and reality is not available to the human being through its own self understanding. It is not therefore surprising that we should find the above contrast with the 'vision of mystery' embodied in Daoism and Zen for whom, as for the Western philosophical approach outlined, it is precisely through the development of self-understanding that the measure of mystery is to be found. But how is this vision related to other forms of what we call 'religion'?

2.

In *The Measure of Things*, David Cooper remarks that the 'vision of mystery' is the 'default' experience of human life and the world: 'That the world presents itself as tinged with mystery is, so to speak, the *default* mode of experiencing it' (p. 346). The Daoist and Zen texts we have looked at do not see this vision as something to be achieved as a goal, but rather it is to be recovered, through the removal of obstacles to self-understanding. Enlightenment for Dogen is not a 'goal for the 'self' to achieve, but rather what manifests itself when we allow what presents life as having a 'goal' for a 'self' to drop away. We are, already, 'Buddha nature' and we would see this as the nature of everything were we to return to our 'original' state, recovering the nature of our primordial way of being in the world. This recovery, experiencing life as constantly given in revealing the world, gives measure to life. The 'problem of the meaning of life' is the experience of a break in the flow of life within which the nature of that flow can be reflectively recovered revealing it as constantly given out of mystery. In that recuperation the 'problem' disappears. Such a break may, of course, precipitate an opposite course, the attempt to *answer* the problem by projecting a graspable measure for life, and so creating ever further obstacles to recovery.

But, it may be said, although in this sense the 'vision of mystery' may appear as what *should* be the 'default' experience of life and the world when the 'problem of life' arises, the manifold forms of religion suggest that, in fact, when the break in unreflective life occurred, it resulted in the projection of a panorama of gods, spirits and other 'supernatural' beings to which human life and the world were subordinated. Far from recovering the nature of primordial experience, it appears the impulse was to see themselves and the world, not as given out of mystery, but as proceeding from the wills and intentions of other 'beings' modeled on human capacities. Cooper remarks 'in the absence of theoretical conceptions, whether of a primitive or sophisticated type, the world would be experienced as a transparent, grace-given epiphany' (*ibid.* p. 347). Are we then to see the notions of gods and spirits as 'theoretical conceptions' which occlude that epiphany? If so, then it might appear that the occlusion has been universal until its recognition in Daoism and Zen forms of Buddhism. If we are not to conceive them in this light, how are we to understand them and their relation to the sense of mystery as the 'default' experience of life and the world?

Wittgenstein, in 'Remarks on Frazer's *Golden Bough*' (in *Philosophical Occasions*, ed. J. Klagge and A. Nordmann, Indianapolis, 1999), objects to Frazer's understanding of religion as the projection of a 'theory' to explain human experience of the world. Frazer saw a progressive development in human culture from magic to religion to science. Each is concerned for him with the explanation of events in the natural world in which human beings pursue their purposes. Eventually they realize that their magical rites do not cause the desired effects and so turn to an explanation in terms of deities: 'there were other beings, like himself, but far stronger, who, *unseen* themselves, directed (the world's) course and brought about all the varied series of events which he had hitherto believed to be dependent on his own magic' (Frazer 1963, p. 75, quoted in D. Z.Phillips, *Religion and the Hermeneutics of Contemplation*, Cambridge 2001, p. 163). But eventually we realize too that prayers and religious rituals are casually inefficacious, and we turn at last to the interrogation of nature: 'the order laid down by science is derived from patient and exact observation of the phenomena themselves' (ibid. p. 932, quoted Phillips p. 163).

Frazer's account presupposes that magic and religion are

engaged in the same project as science: understanding and controlling natural events. Wittgenstein thinks this won't do. Here are people who exhibit wide ranging causal understanding of their environment, without which they would be unable to maintain and reproduce their lives. Must we see their ritual activities and associated discourse of 'gods', 'spirits' and other 'supernatural beings' as an extension of this attempt at causal understanding and control of their environment? Such practices and beliefs don't seem subject to the correction and adjustment in the light of what happens which is characteristic of their practical beliefs and activities. But if not, what account can be given of them?

Wittgenstein remarks of Frazer's account of the sacrifice of the king of the wood at Nemi:'(Frazer) does this in a tone which shows that he feels, and wants us to feel, that something strange and dreadful is happening. But the question 'why does this happen?' is properly answered by saying : Because it is dreadful. That is, precisely that which makes this incident strike us as dreadful, magnificent, horrible, tragic, etc, as anything but trivial and insignificant, is also *that* which has called this incident to life. Here one can only *describe* and say: this is what human life is like ...If a narrator places the priest-king of Nemi and 'the majesty of death' side by side, he realizes that they are the same.

The life of the priest king shows what is meant by that phrase' ('Remarks on Frazer's *Golden Bough*' in Wittgenstein 1993, pp 121-122).

Now, one might immediately ask why 'what makes this incident strike *us* (my emphasis) as dreadful, magnificent, etc' 'is also *that* which has called this incident to life'? Why should I think that how an incident of human sacrifice strikes us shows how it struck the participants and resulted in the rite? Isn't it implausible to suggest this, given that human sacrifice was something the participants expected to occur, indeed saw as a necessary part of social life, rather than something our cultural situation rules out as an intelligible possibility? However, perhaps if we situate Wittgenstein's remarks in a broader context of his thought we may be able to see a way of answering this objection.

In *On Certainty*, Wittgenstein writes 'Giving grounds, … justifying the evidence comes to an end, but the end is not certain propositions striking us immediately as true, i.e. it is not a kind of *seeing* on our part; it is our *acting* which lies at the bottom of the language-game' (Wittgenstein 1969, par. 204). The notion of a language game locates what is said within the context of activity and activity is part of human life. Asking for justification, questioning and doubting are all themselves things we do, and they make sense only under certain circumstances. Wittgenstein writes, 'In certain circumstances, for example, we regard a calculation as sufficiently checked …somewhere we must be finished with justification and then there remains the proposition that *this* is how we calculate' (Wittgenstein 1969, para. 212). Doubting or questioning require the indication of dubitable or questionable circumstances and in their absence nothing which the individual will do can count as such. In this sense there is a certainty of action at the bottom of the language game- this is what we call 'doubting', this 'asserting', this 'settling a question', all within the practice of, say, 'calculating'. That practice is a form of certainty of action: this is what we call 'calculating'. Under certain circumstances, for example, we take as settled what happened in the past, whether someone is in pain, or what caused the explosion. These are what Wittgenstein calls 'primitive reactions': that is, they are primitive in relation to the language game and show the kind of certainty of action which makes the language game what it is. 'The kind of certainty is the kind of language-game' (Wittgenstein 1968, p. 224). Relating to the past, to the feelings, emotions and sensations of others, explaining events, are practices characterized by certainty of action within which we can then understand doubts, questions, as exceptions.

We can describe these forms of certainty of action which are primitive to language games and which make them the language games they are. It is in terms of these forms of certainty of our own language that we can identify the same or similar practices elsewhere.

We acquire a concept of religion in our own culture through its exemplification in some particular religion, but what we acquire is not restricted to that case. We can, as with other language-games, see if other cultures have similar practices so that we can speak of 'religion' there. In terms of what form of 'primitive reaction' might we approach an alien culture in respect of religion?

The case of modern interpretations of the culture of the Moche, a people living on the Northern coast of Peru between the first and eighth centuries Common Era, may be illuminating in this respect. They were not a literate society and there is no continuity of culture to the time of the entry of literate people to record what they said about their religious practices. So the inquirer is left with their own understanding of religion, derived from their own culture and their experience, to see whether and how religious phenomena can be identified in Moche culture. There is clear evidence that a central ceremony of Moche life involved the sacrifice of members of their own elite. Further, funerary ceremonies for elite members involved the ritual performance of sexual acts which are graphically depicted in Moche ceramics. What underlies the identification of the 'sacrifice', and 'sex activity' as religious phenomena and points the way to their interpretation? I will outline Steve Bourget's interpretation of the sexual acts depicted in the Moche ceramics (S. Bourget, *Sex, Death and Human Sacrifice in Moche Religion and Visual Culture*, Austin 2006, chapters 1-3) and Garth Bawden's of the sacrificial rite (G. Bawden, *The Moche*, Oxford 1996, chapters 4-5) and then reflect on what these interpretations suggest as to our understanding of the religious.

We can understand, Bourget suggests, the portrayed rituals of non-vaginal sex between humans and figures associated with physical death (sacrificial victims, mutilated figures, skeletal figures), on the one hand, and vaginal sex with supernatural beings, on the other, in terms of the notion of ritual inversion. The human being, coming into life through sexual reproduction, dies and can then pass into another form of being, the world of the ancestors. This passage is represented by the inverted form of non-reproductive sexual activity. Vaginal sex with supernatural beings and between supernatural animals is, on the other hand, associated with fertility. These portrayed and probably enacted rites show the fertility of humans and of the land and sea as proceeding from the supernatural dimension into which the dead person may pass in becoming an ancestor.

The Moche pyramidal platforms on which the sacrificial rite takes place are symbolic mountains. Moche life and the fertility of the land and its animals depend on the river water which flows from the mountains. Mountains, too, are access routes to the supernatural dimension and it is here that shamanistic initiation, spiritual journeys and encounters with the supernatural can take place. The shaman enters this dimension by way of the mountain entrance represented by the platform structure and probably through trance induced by hallucinogens derived from the San Pedro cactus (Bawden p.155). The dependency of Moche life on the supernatural dimension is now acknowledged in the sacrifice of the human which returns life to it, the blood being poured onto the earth, acknowledging its supernatural dimension as the source of fertility.

In the absence of articulated accounts of Moche representations, what dimension of human life do Bourget and Bawden naturally appeal to in order to make sense of them? What 'primitive reaction' is it which allows our identification of these practices as 'religious'?

Wittgenstein, considering the material in Frazer's book, remarks that 'the awakening of the intellect occurs with a separation from the original *soil*, the original basis of life… (The form of the awakening spirit is veneration)' (*ibid.*, p. 139). The reflective experience of unreflective life incites the 'primitive reaction' of 'veneration', of 'worship'. It is behaviour which we can see as expressing a recognition of dependency, not merely in this or that respect, but of Moche life as a whole on the 'givenness' of human life and its environment. Moche life and the environment which it reveals are recognized in the 'awakening of intellect' as a 'gift'. This is not the recognition of the 'fact' of Moche life: facts have their sense within the world which is given in Moche life. Recognition of life and its world as a 'gift' gives to that life a requirement of a response. It places a normative task on life: to receive life and what happens within it as 'given' within the flow of life itself, and to express this dependency in an explicit form. The expression of a relation to life and what may happen within it as a whole involves the separation from ordinary temporal life exemplified in ritual. Characteristically, the major religious rites take place in a space separated from that of everyday temporal life and involve forms of action divorced from the structure of purposive activity. Ritual involves fixed patterns of behaviour which reflect the relation to what gives sense to the changing life of temporal existence. Rituals too characteristically take place on occasions important for the arrival, maintenance and cessation of life (birth, death, transition to adulthood, entry into reproductive relations, significant times in the agricultural and fishing years, the major climatic changes, and so forth) where the relation to what gives sense to temporality as such finds expression. It is to such a context that the inquirer naturally turns in identifying and understanding the probable interpretation of ritualistic behaviour in the Moche evidence. It is understood as 'veneration', an acknowledgement of, and response to, the experience of Moche life and the world it reveals as a 'gift'.

A relation to the temporal as such, which is embodied in that to the 'givenness' of life and its world, is a relation to the *timeless*. We have seen in Kierkegaard's understanding of Christianity one form this may take. There life and the world as a 'gift' are understood as 'creation' where the timeless is the eternal perspective in terms of which the world can be seen 'as a limited whole' (Phillips ibid, p. 53). That perspective gives sense to the notions of a 'Last Judgement', 'dying to the world', 'redemption', 'original sin', and so forth, to the way Kierkegaard understands the possibilities for meaningful human life. As such an understanding of life's possibilities it is in David Cooper's sense a 'vision', that in terms of which accountability takes place and so is not, to the inhabitant of such a vision, itself accountable. As Wittgenstein says, 'Christianity is not a doctrine, not, I mean, a theory about what has happened and will happen to the human soul, but a way to live within which 'consciousness of sin' is a real event, and so are despair and salvation through faith. Those who speak of such things (Bunyan for instance) are simply describing what has happened to them' (Wittgenstein, *Culture and Value*, 1977, p. 28). Of course, one not occupying such a perspective will not see such accounts as simple 'descriptions ' of what has happened.

But a relation to temporal life as such and so to what happens within it need not only be found in terms of the eternal. Bawden remarks of Andean relations to what we would call nature, which we may assume the Moche shared:' The vital spiritual force that infuses all of nature manifests itself in the spirits of rivers, canals, ocean, and sky, the great mountains that dominate all, and in the variety of discrete sacred places that carry specific supernatural meaning to each social group... These *huacas* are the physical foci for the rituals that mark the interface between the physical and metaphysical aspects of human experience, equally sanctifying the landscape and its inhabitants and linking them in an interdependent relationship, at once tenuous and fundamental' (Bawden 1996, p.65). Once again, such an understanding of the givenness of life and its environment finds its development first and foremost in a way of life. It shows itself in the non-purposive restrictions on behaviour in relation to hunting, fishing and agriculture, for example in taking no more than is needed for the nurture of human life, and in rituals surrounding these activities and the central stages of human life. It manifests itself too in shamanistic experience, in oracles and soothsayers and related phenomena. Here the significance of the temporal does not lie in a relation to a point beyond temporality (the 'absent God'), but rather to the 'sacred' within the temporal itself. Human life and the world it reveals is understood as self-emergence out of mystery (compare Heidegger's account of Greek *physis*). The sacredness of the landscape Bawden refers to is its emergence in life out of mystery which requires therefore recognition in the everyday engagement with it. What gives significance to the temporal here is not a measure beyond it, but a mystery immanent to our lives and the temporal world they reveal. The recognition and celebration of this lies at the heart of the Moche rituals. Human sacrifice returns life to the sacred and so expresses in an extreme form life's dependency on it for the sense it has. Ritual inversion marks the return of the individual at death to the sacred, inverting our entry into temporal life.

This understanding of the emergence of life and its environment out of mystery finds expression in 'mythological' accounts, although we do not, of course, have these in the case of the Moche. The language of myth characteristically violates the principles of accounts of what takes place in time, for example, in providing several conflicting accounts of the emergence of humanity or features of the environment, and in happenings which violate our understanding of the nature of things, as in Aztec myths of people being transformed into monkeys and butterflies. Where such accounts are part of a living culture, they characteristically embody what one might call a dual sense of time. They refer to a 'past' which is nevertheless always 'present' 'behind' what presences in the flow of everyday life. One might say that such accounts are a way of recognizing and bringing out the *giving* of life and the world that that reflection on life reveals. As Lynne Hume remarks on indigenous Australian Dreaming narratives, ' The Dreaming is a living and present reality that continually sustains and energises flora, fauna, and human beings. The life force permeates everything' (*Ancestral Power*, Melbourne, 2002, p. 30). These accounts are a way of reflecting on life and the world it reveals, a way in which the mystery of their emergence is contemplated. It is within that context that we should understand the 'reality' of so called 'supernatural beings'.

'In the beginning, the earth was flat and featureless …Unknown life forms slept blow the surface of the land. Then the great spirits (emerge and) made journeys across the land …moulded and formed the landscape creating rivers, mountains, trees and rocks. They made plants, the animals and all living things- including the people who are descendants of the Spirit Ancestors' (*Us Mob*, Mudrooroo, Sydney, 1995, p. 199). This sounds like an historical narrative- but is it? How are we to understand the 'beginning', the 'emergence' of ancestral powers and their (subsequent?) creation of the landscape, its beings and humanity? We appear to be involved in temporal references, but in what sense, as the originating ancestral powers underlie the present?

Many commentators have remarked on the difference of Dreaming temporality to that of an historical narrative (at least in our common understanding of it). 'In the Dreaming, from any particular point in time, the past may be future and the future may be present. Time does not extend back through a series of pasts, but rather is a 'a vertical line in which the past underlies and is within the present; past and present are mutually compenetrative' (*sic*) ' (Stanner quoted in Hume, p. 38). 'The Dreaming exists independently of the linear time of everyday life and the temporal sequence of historical events. Indeed the Dreaming is as much a dimension of reality as a period of time' (H. Morphy, *Aboriginal Art*, London, 2007, p. 68). And on that dimension of reality, Lynne Hume refers to David Turner's suggestion 'that the dreaming can be termed the 'other side' of 'this side', where 'this side' is the reality we engage with in our everyday lives which we can see and experience, while on the 'other side' there are no fixed forms. 'The Dreaming is a living present reality that continually sustains and energises flora, fauna and human beings ...The Dreaming is 'inside' the immediate present rather than antecedent to it, since the ancestral past and its remnants are within the country' (Hume,pp 51, 70, and 81).

What, then, is the nature of the temporality of the Dreaming accounts according to these interpretations? They are not historical narratives in the sense of depicting datable events. Indeed, in a way they are not about the past more than the present or the future. Rather, they emerge out of an experience of, and reflection on, the living present, the active life of living the cultural forms of a people and revealing and engaging with the reality those cultural forms uncover. Human life is constantly given out of mystery and within that life the reality of the environment and its inhabitants manifest themselves. It is this 'other side' of present experience, its nature as constantly given within which

what is manifests itself, which is addressed in these accounts. The
ancestral powers give the environments, and their inhabitants,
within which aboriginal Australians live, by giving human life
itself (they are *ancestral* spirits, the spirits of the culture), and
this not as 'creation' but as 'creating', by forming the nature of
living life itself. The Dreaming narratives take the 'mythological'
form they do because to speak of this from within life requires a
transgression of language in its ordinary applicability. Myth must
give expression to what does not appear but which makes possible
all appearance: the giving of revelatory life out of mystery. The
point of life then becomes maintaining and expressing a relation
to the mystery of this 'other side'. 'According to Groote Eylandters,
the purpose of life 'on this side' is not only to realize the nature
of the 'other side' while you are here, but also to bring life on
this side into mirrored concert with it' (Hume, p. 51, referring to
Turner's discussion). Characteristically, explicit expression of the
dependency of life on the 'other side' is given in the performance
of ritual activities, while everyday life is itself permeated by its
recognition in preparatory rituals prior to undertaking tasks
and in taking only what is necessary for their performance. As
Epes Brown remarks of a Native American people, 'A complex
system of rules and prescriptions has been passed down so that
the Koyukon will know how to relate respectfully to the natural
world' (Epes Brown, 2001, p. 97). Recognition of the dependency
of life on such an 'other side' can find expression at its extreme in
the human sacrifice and transgressive sexual ritual we saw in the
Moche example.

That these examples do show articulations of the 'vision
of mystery' is suggested by the measure for life and the world,
what is in time, lying not in the timelessness of an eternal
perspective, but in the timelessness of the constant giving of life
and the reality it uncovers. Where life and its environment are
understood as 'creation', there human temporality is referred to
'eternity' and we find an understanding of the past, present and
future as permanently present to God, a position from which the
human present is fully transparent and an ultimate judgement on

life becomes intelligible. One might say it involves a conception of ultimate transparency and so of 'dominion' over what is understood as 'creation'. The human in the image of God is given dominion over the non-human in 'Genesis', although, of course, only in so far as they subordinate themselves to the standard of the eternal in the course of their temporal lives. But the examples we have been considering do not have such a conception of finality. 'Across Oceania ...notions of a completed future were next to non-existent, though of course the belief that the Ancestral state was without end ...was naturally concomitant to views about the abundant life of the spirit realm' (*Religions of Oceania*, T. Swain and G. Trompf, London 1995, p. 161). Nevertheless, these articulations of the 'vision of mystery' differ markedly from the austere ones of Daoism, Zen and the Western philosophical tradition I have outlined. David Cooper stressed the necessity of not 'effing the ineffable' in directing us to mystery, and it may be said that the 'mythological' accounts do just that. But do they?

Mythological accounts are localized. Dreaming accounts, for example, concern the particular people (Yongu, Arrente, and so forth) and their immediate environment and its features, fauna and flora, while it is recognized that other groups have their own Dreaming accounts. They convey, from within life, an articulation of the sense of the giving of life and its environing world in which the focus is on life and the world rather than the mystery which is their arising. The ancestral powers emerge from formlessness, and so out of mystery, but the focus is on their journeys in which, through action and word, they create the people and features of their environing world. The sense of 'environing' is given by the way of life of the people which is given as 'law' by the Ancestral spirits. Indeed, Mudrooroo, himself an indigenous commentator, goes so far as to say 'I would like to suggest that these so-called stories or myths were never primitive attempts to understand the universe, but were narratives which had encoded within them the divine sanctions of the law, the law itself and a commentary on how the law was to be enforced' (*ibid*, p.94). The law, the traditional forms of social relations, productive practices, ceremonies, all that we could call the culture of the people, is articulated and its bindingness on the people finds expression in these accounts, together with the nature of the realities living that life reveals. In this way, the mystery is experienced (the ancestral spirits *emerge*) and conveyed in the account, but is not the focus. That focus is rather on the 'law' in its bindingness on the people, as given by 'ancestral spirits', and the reality which is given in living the 'law'. The ultimate ground for this 'binding' lies in the emergence of the 'spirits' out of mystery, but the focus is on the ancestral spirits and their 'creating ' of the environing world.

Or consider Ancient Egyptian religion with its apparently bewildering catalogue of deities. Richard Wilkinson's *The Complete Gods and Goddesses of Ancient Egypt* (London, 2003) occupies over 170 pages, and is not, despite the title, 'complete' as, for reasons mentioned below, the nature of the Egyptian gods means their number is indeterminate. But if we focus rather on how life lived in terms of this panoply of deities was seen, a more recognizable picture emerges. Human life, its central forms of culture (those in terms of which a meaningful life can be lived and so have authority for Egyptians), and the immediate and wider environments within which that life can be lived, are given 'by the gods'. One recognizes this in a certain comportment in life. Egyptians had no word for religion, for the reason this is so in many ancient and indigenous cultures, that what we would call a 'religious' attitude is pervasive in life. By 'attitude' and 'comportment' I mean to point to Wittgenstein's perception that we recognize 'religion' in 'veneration'. This comportment lies fundamentally in living life as a gift, in giving life and the reality back to 'the gods'. At a symbolic level, this is manifest in offerings to the gods. The king's offering is not a tribute demanded of him, but contains 'something of the freedom that the gods dispense to mankind with the creator's breath' (E. Hornung, *Conceptions of God in Ancient Egypt*, London 1983, p. 203) It is epitomized in the so-called 'negative confession' in which the dead justify themselves before the gods. Here the dead say they have given life to other humans (food to the hungry, drink to the thirsty, clothing for the destitute and provided a boat for those who have none), have not killed or robbed, have not told lies or made distinctions for themselves, and so forth (R. Kemp, *How to Read the Egyptian Book of the Dead*, London 2007, p. 59; G. Shaw, *The Egyptian Myths*, London 2014, p, 192; E. Hornung, *Idea into Image*, Princeton, 1992, p. 141). The essence of this declaration is that the speaker has lived a life recognizing life and reality as a gift, living it in the same spirit as it was given by the gods. To live in this way is to live in accordance with *maat*, 'truth'. As Hornung remarks, 'Maat which came from the gods at creation, returns to them from the hands of men' (E, Hornung 1983, p. 213). In life one lives the god given forms of life and the reality they reveal, returning them to the gods without further purpose or goal in mind. The gods gave for nothing, and we live in their image. To live in *maat* is opposed to *isfet* (injustice, wrong, disorder, unreasonableness), *gereg* (lie), and *khab* (the crooked) (E. Hornung, 1992, p. 136). That these are possibilities for humans shows the nature of what the gift of life entails. We can ignore the gift of life and reality, treating what is given as subject solely to our individual desires and purposes and so live against *maat*. A myth tells of the formation of humans from the tears of the god. The words for 'tear' and 'human' are nearly homophonic in Egyptian and this linguistic accident is used to symbolize the truth of the human condition. We have our lives and the reality they reveal as a gift which as address and claim on us we can fail to acknowledge and so reject. We can live in *maat* or in *isfet*, a life of living in accordance with the gift, or in taking and delusion, a possibility which is absent from the other aspects of creation.

Egyptian religion is the expression of an acute sense of the fragility of meaningful life, and in that, one of a love of life itself, as indeed are all forms of the 'vision of mystery'. Meaningful life is given to the individual; it is not determined by desires and purposes. It is engaged with because it is meaningful and so gives meaning to the individual's life. Such activity, say the pursuit of learning, is the gift of a god, here Djehuti or Thoth. Family life, the life of agriculture, building, crafts of all kinds, and so forth are the gifts of other gods. They are activities concerned with the maintenance, reproduction, governance and celebration of the life which is the gift of the gods. What transpires in the performance of these activities is itself given: the god can give success or failure. In recognizing this, the individual comes into relation to the contingency of the results of human activity. Such activity takes place within a context, which can be ever widened: these too are given and so referred to a god. Most of the Egyptian gods are in fact gods of prescribed locations, towns, kinds of landscape, marshes, deserts, and so forth. As given, what occurred there in human activities depended on the god: that is, what transpired was beyond human control, success, failure, safety or peril was given whatever human desires and purposes may be. Travellers acknowledged the gods of the areas they visited, and this extended to the recognition of Nubian, Asiatic or Libyan gods within their territories. Expedition 'leaders placed themselves under the protection of the deities responsible for the desert tracks or mines or quarries where they worked: the gods of their home town could help little when they were far away' (Hornung, 1983, p. 166). One might pray and make obeisance to these gods, but their 'help' fundamentally lay in recognizing and coming to terms with the contingency intrinsic to human activity, and so to the nature of the 'reality' given, revealed by human life.

The givenness of meaningful human activities and their localized contexts point beyond to wider contexts of what needs recognizing as the 'given' in human life. The small number of gods involved in the various 'creation accounts' mark these aspects. Creation accounts are not historical hypotheses. They are, rather a reflective account from within life on life, a way of recognizing the ways in which that life and the reality it reveals are 'given'. They have the character of referring to a 'past' because what they recount is *always already* presupposed in the unreflective flow of our life. Human life and the reality it reveals are given as a whole and so ultimately are referred to a mysterious arising. This is symbolized in Egyptian myth by the emerging of the gods from the 'Nun', imaged as dark water. The Nun is characterized by negations of the central given conditions of the created world. It is a realm of indeterminate possibility, non-finiteness, absence of illumination and hiddeness. These aspects are spoken of as dyads of male and female gods (Nun/Naunet, Heh/Hauket, Kek/ Kauket, Amun/Amaunet, respectively) since Nun is not mere inertness but the source of the creation of life and reality. From the Nun first emerges, of itself, Atum, the 'lord of totality', and all further gods are Atum's manifestations. Hence, in a sense, all gods are aspects of divinity, *ntr*, the self-emerging giving of life and world. What emerges first is 'totality', the wholeness which characterizes life and world: we live in and of 'reality'. The further gods characterize aspects of this wholeness. The localized contexts of human activities point beyond themselves to the givenness of sky (Nut), earth (Geb), the space between earth and sky (Shu, the air), and moisture (Tefnut). These refer, not to objects of disinterested inquiry, but to the wider contexts within which human life takes place, as experienced in terms of that life. So following the emergence of these gods, proceed the gods of growth and regeneration (Osiris and Isis), and of destruction and disorder (Seth and Nephthys). These are central given aspects of life lived on the earth, beneath the sky. There is no life without death, no order without disorder. Seth is as necessary to the possibility of regeneration and change as is Osiris.

There are different creation accounts, depending on which aspects of the givenness of life and reality one wishes to foreground. According to one account, the elements of creation proceed from Atum, the whole, by creative speech. Here Atum is seen as Ptah, the god of craftsmen and human creation, who brings the world into being by *heka*, 'magic', speech which creates. Here what is emphasized is the fundamental role of language in relation to the 'whole': it is in the givenness of language that the 'whole' is a discursable reality. But if other aspects are to be emphasized, other gods may be synthesized with Atum. Amun can function in this way. The name Amun derives from the verb *jmn* which means 'conceal' or 'be hidden'. In the New Kingdom, Amun is synthesized with Re, the sun-god, and becomes the central deity. Amun-Re is concealment-illumination, which is the form of the manifestation of life and world. There is no illumination but from concealment, and this marks the constant nature of creation in life. Human life is the constant revelation of reality as illuminated out of concealment.

The created world, what emerges from the Nun, is pictured, then, as dual, the realm of human life and that of the gods and the dead, the Duat. The Duat is what is hidden from us but which is necessary for us to have the life and world we have. It is what is recounted in myth. The constant nature of creation finds expression in seeing the emergence of the new day as the 'first occasion', the creation of the world (Hornung, 1983, pp 161-2). The sinking of the sun is pictured as the descent of illumination, Re, into the Duat and so into the source of the gods, the Nun, to be recreated with the sunrise. We, too, in sleep, re-enter the Nun, to be rejuvenated as consciousness and reality are given anew. That the gods, and so our life and world, are finite, they *emerge*, is emphasized by picturing Re's nightly struggle with the snake Apophis, who threatens the end of illumination/concealing, the very manifestation of the world. Apophis must be defeated each night, but always reappears. Here the ultimate fragility of meaningful life in the world is recognized: as ultimately given, it can cease, the gods can return to the Nun from which they emerged (J. Allen, *Genesis in Egypt*, New Haven, 1988, p.14; Hornung 1983, p. 163). Once again, as with the Australian examples, the binding force of god given practices and reality derives from mystery, here the emergence from the Nun. There is a mysterious giving of gods, life and reality. But the focus is not on this mystery, but rather on what is given, the gods and through them the forms of Egyptian culture and the reality they reveal. Myth articulates the 'other side' of everyday life, that which must always already be for it to flow in its taken for granted way. Hence the mythological 'past' which is at the same time behind the presencing of reality in life. What lies' behind' is the giving of forms of life as revelatory of reality, of what is. But behind that lies the mystery imaged in the waters of the Nun.

These myths indeed express a vision of mystery, but one in

terms of a particular cultural life, from within it. They express the binding force of forms of life and the reality they reveal as 'gods' or as 'ancestral spirits'. This is, one might say, a natural extension of language. On the one hand, in speaking of what 'lies behind' everyday experience, we must transgress ordinary language. On the other, we need to reflect that we are claimed by these forms of life and reality, that they have authority for us. Expressing this on the model of human giving and authority, while making clear by the transgressive aspects of the language (there are many different accounts of a 'past', which is nevertheless always, in a sense, present, and whose figures are pictured in alien ways, and so forth) that we are not engaged in giving an 'historical' account, may seem a natural response. It is certainly one we find repeated across cultures. 'Gods' and 'spirits' are the way the authority of forms of life and the reality they reveal appears from *within* living those forms of life. These forms of life are experienced and lived as binding and it is this authority seen from within life that is expressed in speaking of that authority in this way. Forms of life are experienced as 'god-given', as binding on a people, and the source of that authority lies in the emergence of the 'gods' or 'spirits' out of mystery.

3.

But the 'vision of mystery' we have found in Daoist and Zen texts, as well as in the Western philosophical thinkers considered, is not one understood through reference to 'gods' and 'spirits'. It is characterized rather as a *recovery* of something that has been lost. The address of these texts is to people who no longer live within cultural practices whose authority ultimately derives from the mystery that underlies the emergence of gods or ancestor spirits. The Daoist texts address those who have 'lost the Way', Dogen's those who are mired in the illusions of 'discriminating mind', while Heidegger has traced the long history of the West in losing touch with the source of all authority in mystery, culminating in the illusion of the human as its own source. Although Wittgenstein might not have shared these authors understanding of their 'reminders' of mystery as an essential part of a spiritual renewal, he certainly thought that our contemporary culture militated against taking seriously those practices like art and religion which accepted and celebrated the mystery of life and the world, and that were a transformation in culture to take place which rectified this, his own work of reminding us of the mystery of the everyday would cease to have relevance. The 'vision of mystery' articulated in these thinkers brings out something implicit in the religions considered above but not directly addressed. It can become the focus of attention when the specific forms of life concerned lose their authority, the 'gods having fled' as Heidegger might put it, so that the question of the source of authority can manifest itself. There is, of course, no necessity that this will result in a recovery of a 'vision of mystery', as Heidegger's and David Cooper's accounts of the course of Western culture show. The flight of the gods may equally lead to the further concealment of mystery as the source of all authority for human life.

Where the 'gods withdraw', the issue of the authority of life and the world it reveals becomes one about human life itself, a search for a vision, not localized but universal. Whatever the conditions associated with this, whether through forced removal from homelands, wars which destroyed communities and their forms of life sanctioned by the 'gods', or through increased commerce and the movement of people, the search for such a vision becomes manifest in India, China, and the Mediterranean during the second half of the first millennium BCE. Divested of the reference to the gods, the everyday flow of human purposive life is exposed as an issue: what can give it meaning and authority to the 'reality' it claims to reveal? The response in Greece and the subsequent tradition of thought in the West was to see the issue as revealing the intrinsic lack of a measure *within* life and so the need for a relation to a measure beyond human temporal life, a higher reality embodying a timeless standard. If this is to be a measure, it must, at least to a considerable degree, be graspable by us. The world and human life as oriented to the unchangeable as *telos* in Plato and Aristotle, as created by God in terms of the Divine Ideas in the Augustinian vision, or, in the Modern Age, as a rational world, whether by divine dispensation or as the most basic 'fact', understandable in principle by the autonomous rational individual, are forms of this familiar from our Western history, as we have seen. What characterizes these visions is that they are structured in terms of the notions of 'self' and 'other'. The problem of life is seen as one of determining what 'self' is the genuine goal, in terms of the higher reality, for the individual to pursue, and the world is seen as the field of objects within which such a 'self' may be taken as an end. This does not change when the notion of a 'higher reality' is abandoned in what David Cooper calls 'uncompensated humanism' and the measure for human life appears as its capacity for 'choice' (as 'authenticity'). The 'issue' remains the 'true self' which is the goal of life, and the world is understood in relation to this, as the field of 'objects' which may be means, obstacles or an indifferent background to its pursuit.

We see in the east Asian traditions an opposite trajectory. There, the reflective opening of the issue of the measure for life leads to a recovery of a measure internal to life. 'Self' and 'other' are derivative conceptions and presuppose a more fundamental oneness of life and world which is manifest in the primordial nature of the flow of everyday life. That flow is primordially experienced as a *giving*, a mysterious arising. It is this arising out of mystery that is the source of the meaningfulness of life and the authority of the reality it reveals. To live life as this giving, not as a means to a projected future 'self', is to live life for itself, to live in the timeless present. This is, as Zen emphasizes, nothing out of the ordinary, it is everyday life, and yet to be recalled to ourselves in this way is a revelation.

The idea of spiritual development as shedding illusions as to who one already is, to a recovery of how one is *primordially* living in the world, gives a role to reminders of that primordiality and to a reflective appropriation of it. It is this which is developed in the form of 'philosophical reflection' in the Western thinkers I have discussed and which gives to their work the character of a spiritual

practice. It is not, of course, the only such practice nor does it have
any priority, but it is one which can engage and 'disillusion' those
of a certain intellectual temperament. We need to be recalled to
the 'primordial' flow of our everyday lives because it is there we
find the fundamental way in which we and the reality we uncover
are bound together, 'appropriated' as Heidegger would say,
and experienced as *given*, as proceeding from the mystery. This
relation to mystery gives the authority to what we uncover for
us through the authority it gives to our forms of life. Relating to
the mystery gives the measure for life. As this is being recalled
to ourselves, to what we do not know that we know, it can break
in upon us at any time in David Cooper's 'epiphanies', and be
cultivated in the mindful practice of everyday activities. As Zen
reminds us, sweeping the leaves in the garden can be an entry
into *nikon*, the timeless present of the giving of life and world. In
experiencing 'epiphanies' and cultivating what they show us of
our lives, those lives can undergo a transformation, as the young
Wordsworth knew:

'And I have felt
A presence that disturbs me with the joy
Of elevated thoughts; a sense sublime
Of something far more deeply interfused,
Whose dwelling is the light of setting suns,
And the round ocean and the living air,
And the blue sky, and in the mind of man:
A motion and a spirit, that impels
All thinking things, all objects of all thoughts,
And rolls through all things. Therefore am I still
A lover of the meadows and the woods,
And mountains, and of all that we behold
From this green earth; of all the mighty world
Of eye, and ear,-both of what they half create,
And what perceive; well pleased to recognize
In nature and the language of sense,
The anchor of my purest thoughts, the nurse,

The guide, the guardian of my heart, and soul
Of all my moral being.'
(William Wordsworth, *Lines composed a few miles above Tintern Abbey*).

But the relation of what we call 'art' and 'literature' to a 'vision of mystery' needs discussion elsewhere.

Bibliography

Abe, Maseo, *A Study of Dogen*, Albany, 1992.

Allen, j. *Genesis in Egypt*, New Haven, 1988.

Ames, R.T. and Hall, D.L., *Dao De Jing*, New York, 2003.

Bawden, G., *The Moche*, Oxford, 1996.

Bourget, S, *Sex, Death and Human Sacrifice in Moche Religion and Visual Culture*, Austin, 2006.

Brown, Epes, *Teaching Spirits*, Oxford, 2001.

Child, W., *Wittgenstein*, Abingdon, 2011.

Cooper, D.E., *Heidegger*, London, 1996.

Cooper, D. E., *Existentialism*, Oxford, 2000.

Cooper, D.C., *The Measure of Things*, Oxford, 2002.

Cooper, D. E., *World Philosophies*, Oxford, 2003.

Cooper, D.E., *A Philosophy of Gardens*, Oxford, 2006.

Cooper, D.E., *Convergence with Nature*, Totnes, 2012.

Cooper, D.E., *Sunlight on the Sea*, no place of publication, 2013.

Cooper, D.E., *Senses of Mystery*, Abingdon, 2018.

Cooper, D.E., *Animals and Misanthropy*, Abingdon, 2018.

Cooper, D. C., Interview in 3ammagazine *The Measure of Things*, at 3ammagazine.com.

Davis, B. W., 'Forms of Emptiness in Zen' in *A companion to Buddhist Philosophy*, Oxford, 2013.

Graham, A.C., *Chuang-tzu: The Inner Chapters*, Indianapolis, 2001.

Heidegger, M., *Being and Time*, trans. J. MacQuarrie and E. Robinson, Oxford, 1967.

Heidegger, M., *Identity and Difference*, trans. J. Stambaugh, New York 1969.

Heidegger, M., *On Time and Being*, trans. J. Stambaugh, London 1972.

Heidegger, M., *The End of Philosophy*, trans. J. Stambaugh, London, 1975.

Heidegger, M., *Basic Writings*, ed. D. Krell, London, 1978.

Heidegger, M., *The Basic Problems of Phenomenology*, trans. A. Hofstadter, Bloomington, 1982.

Heidegger, M., *Basic Questions of Philosophy*, trans. R.Rojewicz and A.Schuwer, Bloomington, 1994.

Heidegger, M., *The Fundamental Concepts of Metaphysics*, trans. W. McNeill and N.Walker, Bloomington, 1995.

Heidegger, M., *Introduction to Metaphysics*, trans. G.Fried and R.Polt, New Haven, 2000.

Heidegger, M., *The Heidegger Reader*, ed. G. Figal, Boomington, 2009.

Heidegger, M., *Bremen and Freiburg Lectures*, trans. A. Mitchell, Bloomington 2012.

Heidegger, M., *Country Path Conversations*, trans. B.W.Davis, Bloomington, 2016.

Hornung, E., *Conceptions of God in Ancient Egypt*, London, 1983.

Hume, L., *Ancestral Power*, Melbourne, 2002.

Kasulis, T., *Zen Action Zen Person*, Honolulu, 1987.

Kierkegaard, S. *Journals*, trans. H. and E. Hong, Indianapolis, 1967.

Kierkegaard, S., *Fear and Trembling*, trans. H. and E. Hong, Oxford, 1983.

Kierkegaard, S., *The Concept of Irony*, trans. H. and E. Hong, Oxford, 1989.

Kiekegaard, S., *Concluding Unscientific Postscript*, trans. H. and E. Hong, Oxford, 1992.

Linnels, B.R., *'Nei-yeh' at www.gutenberg.org/files/38585 pdf/38585-pdf.pdf*

Morphy, H., *Aboriginal Art*, London, 2007.

Mudrooroo, *Us Mob*, Sydney, 1995.

Okumara, S., *Reading Genjokoan*, Somerville, 2011.

Phillips, D.Z., *Religion and the Hermeneutics of Contemplation*, Cambridge, 2001.

Rhees, R. 'Wittgenstein's Builders' in *Discussions of Wittgenstein*, London, 1970.

Rhees, R., *Wittgenstein and the Possibility of Discourse*, Oxford, 1998.

Roth, H.D., *Original Tao*, New York, 1999.

Swain, T. and Trompf, F., *Religions of Oceania*, London, 1995.

Tanahashi, K., *Enlightenment Unfolds*, Boston, 1999.

Tanahashi, K., *Beyond thinking*, Boston, 2004.

Tanahashi, K. and Levitt, P., *The Essential Dogen*, Boston, 2013.

Wang, K., *Reading the Dao*, London, 2011.

Wilkinson, R., *The Complete Gods and Goddesses of Ancient Egypt*, London, 2003.

Wittgenstein, L., *Tractatus Logico-Philosophicus*, London, 1961.

Wittgenstein, L., *Lectures and Conversations on Aesthetics, Psychology and Religious Belief*, ed. C. Barrett, Oxford 1967.

Wittgenstein, L., *Zettel*, trans. G.E.M. Anscombe, Oxford, 1967.

Wittgenstein, L., *On Certainty*, trans. D. Paul and G.E.M. Anscombe, Oxford, 1969.

Wittgenstein, L., *Culture and Value*, trans. P. Winch, Oxford, 1980.

Wittgenstein, L., *Philosophical Occasions*, ed. J. Klagge and A. Nordmann, Indianapolis, 1999.

Wittgenstein, L. *Philosophical Investigations*, trans. G.E.M. Anscombe, P. Hacker and J. Schulte, Oxford, 2009. (Part 2 is 'Philosophy of Psychology: a Fragment').

Printed in Great Britain
by Amazon

84407149R00108